The Greek Patristic
View of Nature

Coniugi meae dilectissimae quae vitam
veram vivit me modo scribente

D S Wallace-Hadrill

The Greek Patristic
View of Nature

Manchester University Press

Barnes & Noble Inc., New York

© 1968 D S Wallace-Hadrill

Published by
Manchester University Press
316–324 Oxford Road
Manchester 13

GB SBN 7190 0350 4

Barnes & Noble, Inc.
105 Fifth Avenue
New York, N.Y. 10003

Printed in Great Britain by
Butler & Tanner Ltd
Frome and London

Contents

43013

Preface

This is a designedly one-sided book. It has seemed to me worth trying to say something, however briefly, to counteract the idea that Christianity necessarily ignores this world in favour of the next; that it necessarily involves denigration of the world and the flesh, and inevitably completes the satanic triad by associating them with the devil; that beauty is connected in the Christian mind with moral debility, and is therefore to be shunned. This book sets out to suggest that such views are not necessarily an integral part of Christian belief by adducing evidence from some of the Greek fathers of the first four centuries A.D. To cover the whole ground and set the problems involved in perspective and balance would call for time, space and scholarship beyond my command. A complete picture would go far into the history of ethics to discuss the evidence presented by early monasticism and its associated rigorist and ascetic practices. These important fields of study have been the subject of what Professor F. L. Cross has called 'an immense literature', which I mention here only in order to make clear that I am aware that the attitudes to nature illustrated in this book are not the only attitudes there are.

The view that to many of the Greek fathers the world appeared interesting, enjoyable and important has been less emphasised, and apart from a few monographs which have come to my notice, is discussed mainly in notes attached to patristic texts. These are confined largely to elucidation of the literary sources used by the authors in question, an aspect of their work with which I am only indirectly concerned in this book. In the interests of brevity, I have confined my attention almost entirely to the primary sources. In this I have received great help from the Librarians and Library staffs of universities other than my own, especially those of the University of Durham and of King's College, London, who have shown much kindness to a *vagans* who has had to work as best he can in places whither the ministry of the Church of England has led him. I am very grateful to them for their help.

Throughout this book the following abbreviations are used:

G.C.S.	*Die griechischen christlichen Schriftsteller der ersten drei Jahrhunderte* (Leipzig)
P.G.	Migne, *Patrologia Graeca*
P.L.	Migne, *Patrologia Latina*
C.S.E.L.	*Corpus Scriptorum Ecclesiasticorum Latinorum* (Vienna)
S.C.	*Sources chrétiennes* (Paris)

In the first of his Wiles Lectures delivered in Belfast in 1963, Professor E. R. Dodds describes 'the progressive devaluation of the cosmos in the early Christian centuries (in other words, the progressive withdrawal of divinity from the natural world), and the corresponding devaluation of ordinary human experience'.[1] He traces the growth of this pessimism with reference largely to the non-Christian writers of the age, but with some reference also to the Christians, relying mainly upon Clement of Alexandria, Origen and Gregory of Nyssa among the Greeks, and Tertullian and Augustine among the Latins. Some twenty further Latin and Greek fathers are mentioned in passing or are the subject of reference in footnotes. It is the purpose of the present book to re-examine some of the writings of the Greek fathers of the first four centuries in order, it is hoped, to elucidate a little further what they say about the physical world in which they lived. As we follow the Greek fathers over this ground we shall find ourselves constantly on the boundaries of other territories upon which, inviting though they may be, we must not trespass. Study of the nature of the physical world could lead, as it does in R. A. Norris, *God and World in Early Christian Theology* (London, 1966), into the realm of metaphysics, but if we allow ourselves to glance over this boundary, it will be only in order to take our bearings. Study of the place of man in his biological setting must lead to some account of his position, as the fathers saw it, midway between pure spirit and pure

[1] *Pagan and Christian in an Age of Anxiety* (Cambridge 1965), p. 37.

matter, and here again, we shall not stray too far into
the region of the spirit. Nor shall we follow too far the
path which leads from man's sensory experience into
the field of ethics, nor the path from patristic exegesis of
natural references in the scriptures to consideration of
their methods of exegesis at large. These and similar
fields of enquiry we shall acknowledge as may be needful and largely pass by. The Christian stood at his
door and looked out at a universe of earth, air, water,
plants, animals, insects and birds; skies and stars and
sun and moon; pleasant spring growth and destroy-
ing winter storms; health and sickness; and amidst
these, man. How much of it interested him? What
in all this did he find important, and in what sense
did he find it important? What was man's place in
it?

It must be recognised at once that on these questions
the Greek fathers do not all speak with one voice. They
are individuals, often sharply differentiated in ability,
power of observation and education, just as individual
works were written for very different purposes. There is
a great gulf between the strange allegorisings of Hermas
and the detailed physical analysis of Basil; between
the theological reference of Origen's physical observations and the unexpectedly objective observations of
Nemesius, who, for all his theological purpose, comes
nearer than any to writing like a man of science;
between the indoor manner of Eusebius, who normally
sees only as much of nature as can be seen through his
study window, and the outdoor manner of Clement of
Alexandria, who knows what it is like jumping a ditch
or smelling the dung in a farmyard. They differ too
in the extent of their knowledge: Basil clearly knows
something of anatomy; Theophilus of Antioch clearly
does not. A few, notably Nemesius, are familiar with,
and are even prepared on occasions to question, primary
sources such as Aristotle and Galen; the majority rely

upon manuals of instruction based on the work of the great pioneers of research. Gregory of Nyssa displays a remarkable power of natural description quite distinct from the more rhetorically effective passages of Gregory of Nazianzus. We are dealing not with a school but with individual men, and men who were, in the modern sense, amateurs.

Two of the Greek fathers, Basil and Nemesius, seem to have undergone medical training, though neither practised the art; others, trained in philosophy, had to varying degrees studied the nature of the physical world,[1] but none is a scientist in the sense in which the term could be used of Aristotle or Theophrastus, and none receives a favourable report in histories of science. Referring briefly to the fathers as a whole, Latin as well as Greek, Charles Singer says that their interests were not conducive to the study of phenomena.[2] His *History of Biology* passes from Galen to the thirteenth century in a few pages, dismissing in a single sentence the ecclesiastical authors who 'with edification always in view, produce moralised and sometimes illustrated animal stories which exhibit no intelligent observation and are often childish to the verge of imbecility'.[3] If this generalised condemnation is based upon animal stories found in the lives of the desert fathers[4] it has something to commend it; to describe in these terms the natural observations of Basil, Gregory of Nyssa and Nemesius is to be guilty of serious exaggeration. What is true is that the fathers did not advance the study of natural phenomena by their own researches. They were bishops, not scientists. During the four centuries of scientific

[1] See H-I. Marrou, *Histoire de l'Éducation* (Paris 1948), pp. 232-4, for the general scientific culture of the age.

[2] A *Short History of Science* (Oxford 1941).

[3] Revised ed. 1950, p. 62.

[4] e.g. Rufinus, *Historia Monachorum*; Dionysius Exiguus, *Vita S. Pachomii*; Palladius, *Historia Lausiaca*; *Vita Divi Hieronymi;* etc.

advance which ended with Galen, writes Professor
Benjamin Farrington, 'there had arisen a conception of
science as a cycle of liberal studies for a privileged
minority. Science had become a relaxation, an adorn-
ment, a subject for contemplation'.[1] It was in this
relaxed setting that the fathers became acquainted with
scientific disciplines, and what knowledge they had
attained was used by them for homiletic or expository
purposes. Indeed, we find them often expressing a low
opinion of scientific study pursued for its own sake.

This is interesting in view of the fact that their low
estimate of science did not stem from any feeling that
the work of the scientist in any way threatened or under-
mined that of the theologian, nor from any serious
ignorance of the nature of scientific enquiry. Even
Theophilus of Antioch, not always the most perceptive
of the Greek fathers, could see that scientific conclusions
were less a matter of logical certainty than of experimental probability.[2] Gregory of Nyssa recognises that
scientific thinking is not a matter of speculation; it
requires training—one is not born with the knowledge
of how to handle a theodolite.[3] Scientific advances
are achieved, he says, through experiment: 'Medical
writers learnt by dissection the position of our bodily
organs.'[4] Gregory of Nazianzus puts his position clearly:

If you understand orbits and periods, waxings and wanings,
settings and risings, degrees and minutes, you have not
arrived at a knowledge of the realities themselves, but only
at an observation of certain movements, from which, when
confirmed by longer practice and by collating the observations of many others into a single generalised statement,
is deduced a law. This process has acquired the name of
science.[5]

---

[1] *Greek Science*, 2nd ed. (London 1949), p. 302.
[2] *ad Autol.*, iii.16, 17.
[3] *Antirrhet. contra Eunom.* (= *c. Eunom.*, xii.b).
[4] *de virg.*, xxiii; *de hom. opif.*, xxx.1.   [5] *Orat.*, xxviii.29.

Gregory here shows that he understands very well how a scientific law comes to be formulated, and also the reason why he does not consider such work to be of importance: it does not go far enough. 'You have not arrived at a knowledge of the realities themselves.' Gregory here stands in a philosophical tradition which can be traced back as far as Plato's argument in the *Meno* and the *Laws*, that no exact knowledge of phenomena is possible, an argument reinforced for the Christian by Paul's denunciation of the wisdom of this world. 'Knowledge of the realities themselves' can only come by revelation, a point made constantly by the fathers, and not to be confused with the ubiquitous hostility to philosophical speculation. Some scientific conclusions can only be achieved by speculation, such as the question how the earth is supported in space, a question which Basil therefore declares to be unanswerable with certainty.[1] But even when the conclusion has been reached by a process of patient observation and collation of results, the scientist has not reached an understanding of the reality. This they had learnt from Plato. Not all, however, had quite taken Origen's point that the phenomena of nature have not only as little, but also as much significance as the bare word of the scriptures, and that scientific understanding of nature has as little and as much importance as the historical understanding of scripture. Neither the historical narrative, nor the natural object was, in Origen's view, to be rejected as useless.[2] Often, however, the scientific study of nature was so rejected. Characteristic is Tatian's scornful gibe at astronomers: 'gaping at the sky, you tumble into pits'. 'How can I believe one who tells me that the sun is a red-hot mass and the moon an earth? Such assertions are mere word-spinning, not sober exposition of truth.'[3] This is the accusation of unverifiable

[1] *Hex.*, i.8.21b. [2] See below, p. 121.
[3] *Orat. ad Graec.*, xxvi.

speculation. 'What is the use of measuring the earth
or knowing the positions of the stars and the course
of the sun?'[1] This is the more important accusation
of triviality and irrelevance. Eusebius, like many of
the fathers, sets out at some length the mutual contra-
dictions of Greek cosmologists, and concludes that such
enquiries are irrelevant from the point of view of right
conduct,[2] an argument in which he is followed closely
by Theodoret, who caps the conclusion with a tag from
Aeschylus, 'In what is useless, labour not in vain.'
Scientific enquiries, he says, are like writing on water
or drawing water in a sieve.[3] Basil classifies winged
creatures under four headings, schizoptera, dermoptera,
ptilota and coleoptera. He uses this technical terminology as though it leaves a nasty taste in the mouth,
referring to 'those who have dug up new words' to
classify varieties. He claims that the Levitical classification of birds into two classes, pure and impure, is
superior to the Aristotelian classification.[4] But he has
got Aristotle's classification wrong, whether through
his own fault or that of an intermediary source. His
absurd dismissal of Aristotelian terminology is unex-
pected on the lips of one who manifestly regarded this
kind of enquiry as interesting and important. It is
possible that we might take it as the slightly embarrassed
disclaimer of a learned man finding himself using
difficult words to an unlearned congregation. Gregory
of Nyssa describes Basil delivering these homilies on the
six days of creation: 'He was addressing a crowded
church and had to modify his exposition in order to suit
their understanding, with workmen and women present,
and a mob of boys.'[5] But Basil should have made sure

[1] *Orat. ad Graec.*, xxvii.   [2] *Prae. Evang.* xv.8.808c.
[3] *Graec. affect. cur.*, iv.24, 25. The quotation from Aeschylus is
found also in Clem. Alex., *Strom.*, v.1.5.
[4] *Hex.*, viii.3.169c–172a.
[5] *in Hex.*, *P.G.*, 44.66a.

of understanding Aristotle before permitting himself
the luxury of a sneer. He returns later to the contrast
between scientific probability and revealed truth:
'there have been many mutually contradictory opinions
about the shape of the earth, about which the Penta-
teuch says nothing. Moses did not trouble about
estimating the perimeter of the earth, nor did he
speculate about eclipses of the moon. The information
is useless to us.'[1] One should not wear oneself out, says
Gregory of Nyssa, following every track of footprints
left by truth.[2] This sounds as though Gregory could
admit that truth, 'the knowledge of the reality itself',
is attainable by scientific procedure, but before long
he is asserting that rational certainty, as the philosopher understands it, is not to be attained when explain-
ing natural phenomena.[3] Only probability, not truth:
therefore useless to those who seek the truth. So runs
the argument over and over again. But it had not been
the argument of Origen, nor of Clement of Alexandria
before him. Writing of divinely given knowledge in
various spheres of human activity and experience,
Clement says that he includes natural science, 'which
treats of the phenomena of the world of sense'.[4] For him,
φυσικὴ θεωρία, the contemplation of nature, was the
first stage by which the soul attained the knowledge of
God. Along with other branches of philosophy, it is
'conducive to piety, being a kind of preparatory training
for those who attain to faith through demonstration'.[5]
Origen, too, allows that profane knowledge can be
inspired by God, specifying geometry and its derivative,
architecture, and the knowledge of natural phenomena
such as animals, the flight of birds and the differences
between the cries of animals.[6] In his commentary on the
song of Solomon, Origen classifies the four branches of

[1] *Hex.*, ix.1.188c–189a.   [2] *in Hex., P.G.*, 44.97a.
[3] ibid., 109c.   [4] *Strom.*, ii.2.5.1.
[5] ibid., 1.5.28.   [6] *Hom. in Num.*, xviii.2.3.

knowledge, ethical, physical, mystical and logical. The
first three fall in this order, with the study of physical
phenomena lying second in the scheme, and logic inter-
penetrates all three.[1] Of the kind of thing studied in
physical science, Origen elsewhere specifies botany,
zoology and meteorology.[2] Origen makes plain, however, that physics, having shown the causes of things,
should then be forsaken, so that the student can hasten
on to what is lasting and eternal. The man in pursuit
of wisdom will not delay over the study of phenomena.
If the Alexandrian tradition permitted the study of
natural science, it nevertheless regarded science as a
preliminary discipline preparatory for higher and more
important studies, and when the Greek fathers talk
about science as an intellectual discipline, this is the
best they can say for it. The point of interest is not,
however, their rather low estimate of science, but the
fact that their practice was so markedly at variance with
their theory. We pass now to a review of some of
the things they say, not about science, but about the
phenomena which are the subject-matter of science.
Here we find that they exhibit an interest in the structure of the physical world and its inhabitants which in
many cases amounts to fascination. The excerpts from
and references to their writings which follow are drawn
from works in which the subject under discussion con-
cerns the spiritual life of man, devotional, mystical,
biblical, liturgical, theological. Yet constantly we find
the fathers drawing attention to the natural world, not
in general terms but in extraordinary detail, not always
briefly but sometimes at great length and with doubt-
ful relevance to their professed subject. Their opinions
are seldom original and are not seldom manifestly
wrong; their knowledge of the physical world reflects
that of their age. What we are concerned with is not

[1] *Comm. in Cant.*, Prol. iii.
[2] *Hom. in Num.*, xii.1.1.

their rightness, but their interest. Nature was important to them.

What follows is grouped under four main headings: Astronomy and Cosmology; Meteorology; Botany and Horticulture; Zoology. Patristic treatment of human anatomy and physiology and of medicine, is considered in the next chapter.

Astronomy and cosmology

Basil is predictably unimpressed by astronomers, but appreciates the extent of their enquiries: 'Astronomers pay such attention to vain objects that they blind themselves to the truth.' They measure the distance of the stars, draw up a list of those which shine in the northern and southern hemispheres, they divide the boreal zone ($\beta\acute{o}\rho\varepsilon\iota o\nu$ $\pi\lambda\acute{a}\tau o\varsigma$) and the circle of the zodiac into numerous sections, they observe with great care the rising of the stars, their positions and their setting, their movement, and the duration of the moving stars each in its own orbit.[1] Gregory of Nyssa is filled with wonder at

the reverse planetary motion, the so-called zodiac graven obliquely upon the pole, whereby astronomers observe the motion of bodies revolving in an opposite direction, the differences of size and of brightness between stars, their risings and settings that follow undeviatingly according to the time of year, the conjunctions of planets, the orbits of those that pass below, the eclipses of those above, the obumbrations of the earth, the reappearance of the eclipsed bodies, the many changes of the moon, the motion of the sun midway between the poles, when the disc of the moon, so they say, passes before him,[2]

all of which, Basil justly observes in a letter to Amphilochius, is too much for the human eye to take in

[1] *Hex.*, i.4.12b.
[2] *Antirrhet. c. Eunom.* (= *c. Eunom.*, xii.b).

B

at a single glance.[1] Basil is prepared to stand in wonder at the heavens, but 'geometry, arithmetic, study of solid bodies, this famous astronomy, all this empty labour, what do they lead to?'[2]

The contrary motion of the planets is axiomatic in patristic understanding of astronomy. Observe, says Origen, the constant revolution of the fixed stars, the converse motion of the planets.[3] Gregory of Nyssa draws attention to the harmony of the whole system, 'the unity which results even from opposite movements in the orbits', in which the inner stars revolve in a direction contrary to that in which the fixed stars move.[4] Basil, possibly familiar with Aristotle's attempt in the *Physics* to demonstrate the eternity of the heavens by the circular movement of the stars, is of the opinion that the fact that circular orbits have no beginning geometrically, does not of necessity imply that stars had no beginning in time. A circle, he argues, can only be defined by reference to a centre and a radius: it has, in fact, a geometrical starting point.[5] Theophilus perhaps refers to variation of planetary orbits when he writes that the greatest stars signify the prophets, because unlike the planets, they do not deviate in their courses.[6] In the same way he observes 'the varying conjunctions of the Pleiads and Orion, of Arcturus and the other stars'.[7] Origen records the view of Plato and the Pythagoreans, that planets would eventually return to their original positions and effect a repetition of the same cycle of terrestrial events, but he had already written that the cause of the final conflagration would be moral, not

---

[1] *Ep.*, 233.   [2] *Hex.*, i.3.9c.

[3] *c. Cels.*, viii.52. The fixed stars move from east to west, *c. Cels.*, i.23.   [4] *de infant.*, also *c. Eunom.*, i.27.

[5] *Hex.*, i.3.9b. Basil had previously given the common definition of a circle: a plane figure described by a single line.

[6] *ad Autol.*, ii.16.

[7] ibid., i.6.

'cycles and planetary periods'.[1] Comets, in the view of Gregory of Nyssa, may not be stars at all: 'We are told by students that those gleams which follow each other so fast through the air at night, which some call shooting stars, are nothing but the air itself streaming into the upper regions of the sky under pressure. They say that the fiery track is traced along the sky where those blasts ignite in the aether.'[2] Clement of Alexandria also says that comets are produced by atmospheric changes.[3] Of the speed at which stars move, Gregory of Nyssa writes that those further from the earth move at a greater speed than those which are nearer.[4]

The use of astronomy as a navigational aid is referred to by many of the Greek fathers,[5] but to my knowledge there is no detailed account of its use.

Origen, though a little hesitant for lack of authoritative statement by the Church, is of the opinion that planets may possess souls.[6] The planets exhibit orderly motion, which suggests to him that they are not irrational beings,[7] and against Celsus he maintains that stars may be rational and virtuous.[8] Elsewhere he speaks of them as placed in order in the heavens according to their rank.[9] Eusebius rejects with scorn what he

---

[1] c. Cels., v.21; iv.11, 12.

[2] de virg., xi; in Hex., P.G., 44.96d–97a. cf. Aristotle, Meteor., i.4.

[3] protrept., x.102.4.

[4] in Hex., P.G., 44.120a.

[5] e.g. Clem. Alex., Strom., vi.16.143.1; Origen, de princ., iii.1.18; Basil, Hex., vi.4.125d; Cyril of Jerus., Cat., ix.8.; Theodoret, de prov., iv., P.G., 83.616c.

[6] de princ., praef.x.

[7] ibid., i.7.3, 4.

[8] c. Cels., v.10; Comm. in Joh., ii.3.

[9] Hom. in Jesu Nave, xxv.4; cf. Comm. in Gen., iii.5. Tatian may have the same idea in mind in writing of 'a spirit in the stars', Orat. ad Graec., xii, and Novatian in writing of the world as being guided by the angels and the stars, de Trin., viii; an astrological reference is unlikely. cf. Clem. Alex., Strom., vi.17.148.2., 'administrative powers'.

describes as the Greek notion that the stars are red-hot masses of metal fixed in the sky like studs and plates.[1]

'What is the use of knowing the causes of the sun's movement?' asks Clement of Alexandria,[2] and he has little indeed to say of the sun, other than observing its light coming through windows and crevices[3] and its heat causing fire when passed through a glass vessel full of water.[4] The brilliance of the sun is, of course, matter for widespread comment.[5] Gregory of Nyssa writes of sunlight being bearable to the human eye because filtered through the intervening atmosphere,[6] and Gregory of Nazianzus finds it bearable when reflected in water.[7] Basil follows Aristotle in regarding the solar halo as an indication of moisture in the atmosphere,[8] a phenomenon which may be in the mind of Gregory of Nyssa when he writes 'the body of the sun is plainly imaged by the whole disc that surrounds it, and he who looks at the sun argues, from what he has seen, the existence of the whole solid substratum'.[9] Gregory also describes the shadow of the earth cast by the sun's light:

those skilled in astronomy tell us that the whole universe is full of light, and that darkness is made to cast its shadow by the interposition of the earth's body; and that this darkness is shut off from the rays of the sun in the shape of a cone, in

---

[1] *Prae. Evang.*, vii.11.319d.

[2] *Strom.*, vi.11.93.1.

[3] ibid., vii.3.21.7; cf. Origen, *de princ.*, i.1.6.

[4] *Strom.*, vi.17.149.1.

[5] Barnabas, *Ep.*, v.10; Origen, *de princ.*, i.1.5; Theophilus, *ad Autol.*, i.5; Eusebius, *Dem. Evang.*, iv.6; Basil, *ad nean.*, ix; Cyril of Jerus., *Cat.*, vi.29; ix.8; xii.13., etc.

[6] *Antirrhet. c. Eunom.*, (= *c. Eunom.*, xii.b).

[7] *Orat.*, xxviii.3.

[8] *Hex.*, vi.4.125b; cf. Aristotle, *Meteor.*, iii.3.372b. Basil notes that the same is true of the moon, and says that these phenomena are known as ἀνθηλίους, as in Plutarch, *de plac. phil.*, iii.6.

[9] *c. Eunom.*, viii.1.

accordance with the figure of a spherical body, and behind it. The sun, exceeding the earth many times in size, enfolds it on all sides with its rays and unites the concurrent streams of light at the apex of the cone.[1]

It was the heat of the sun, according to Basil, which dispersed the water originally covering the earth. Basil argues back from the way in which the sun is observed to evaporate water to the enormous quantity of water there must have been originally, in order to leave the present volume of water unevaporated. The Peripatetics were mistaken, he says, in denying the original abundance of water, and in saying that the sun is not hot by nature, but only has heat generated in it by its rapid revolutions; and having said this, continues Basil, they are inconsistent in maintaining that the sea is salt by reason of the sun's great heat consuming its lighter particles.[2] Basil maintains that the heat of the sun would be too great for the earth if it stood still in the heavens; its movement ensures the maintenance of good order in the world, to which Theodoret adds the further point that there is an important balance between the heat of the sun and the humidity of the atmosphere.[3] According to Origen the effect of the sun on an object is also determined by the nature of the object itself, some objects being illuminated (bleached?) and some darkened and hardened with heat.[4]

The origin and creation of the sun gives rise to some speculation. Celsus ridicules the absurdity of the author of Genesis in talking of 'days' before describing the creation of the sun, a point which Origen puts aside with a reference to those who go no deeper into scripture

[1] de hom. opif., xxi.3; in Hex., P.G., 44.93ab, 77b.

[2] Hex., iii.7.69ab, 72a. Aristotle, Meteor., 1.3.341a, ii.2.355a.

[3] Hex., iii.7.69c; Theodoret, Graec. affect. cur., iv.64. cf. Clem. Alex., Protrept., i.5.1. 'the violence of fire is softened by the atmosphere'.

[4] Comm. in Cant., ii.2 (Cant. i.69). cf. Hom. in Exod., xiii.14, where fire has the twofold effect of illuminating and burning.

than its apparent or surface meaning.[1] But Origen himself had been uneasy on the same point: 'Who that has understanding will suppose that the first, second and third day, and the evening and the morning, existed without a sun and moon and stars, and that the first day was also without a sky?'[2] Basil notes the point: 'Some say it is the warmth of the sun which is the cause of germination, but germination began before the sun was created,'[3] and elsewhere in the *Hexaemeron* he offers these explanations of the difficulty. The sky, he says in Book ii, was not yet complete, 'not yet having received the beauty proper to it, illuminated by neither sun nor moon and uncrowned yet by the choirs of stars',[4] by which he may mean what Gregory of Nyssa expressed in more formal terms when he wrote of an invisible world before its creation being in a state of pure potentiality, possessing existence but not colour or other visible qualities.[5] Later in Book ii Basil says that day and night were not originally caused by the circuit of the sun at all, but by the alternation of a different and more primitive light and darkness instituted by God. The world could be said to be good, that is beautiful, even before the creation of our day and night, because beauty depends not upon light but upon symmetry of parts.[6] In Book iv Basil says that the sun was created by God later than the earth to prevent our thinking that it was the sun which dried the earth,[7] an opinion which is hardly consistent with his argument in Book iii that the sun has evaporated vast quantities of water from the

[1] *c. Cels.*, vi.60.

[2] *de princ.*, iv.1.15.

[3] *Hex.*, v.1.96ab.   [4] *Hex.*, ii.1.29b.

[5] *in Hex.*, *P.G.*, 44.77d–80a. cf. the remark of Theophilus that, unlike the firmament, the heavens are invisible to us, *ad Autol.*, ii.13.

[6] *Hex.*, ii.7.48b. cf. Plotinus, *Enn.*, i.6.1. As an afterthought Basil does allow that light is not only beautiful, but useful too.

[7] *Hex.*, iv.5.88c.

surface of the earth since its creation.[1] Gregory of
Nyssa contributes two points to the discussion. He
envisages the first moment of the act of creation as
bringing into existence everything, even light, though
the latter was still obscured from vision. It required
three days to set in order this primitive light because of
the enormous distances between the heavenly bodies.[2]
Earlier he had observed that the nature of fire is such
that it moves upwards at great speed. When fire was
first released from the earth it rushed upwards and
found itself drawn into orbit round the earth.[3]

Theophilus claims that the sun is the smallest of the
stars,[4] which is not quite the same as the remark of
Cyril of Jerusalem that the sun is 'a small work of God'.[5]
The reference at Genesis i.16 to two great lights means
only that the sun and moon are relatively great, writes
Basil, yet their circumference is sufficient for them to
illuminate the atmosphere over earth and sea. Distance
affects the apparent size of objects because of the weakness of man's power of vision. The power of the sun
indicates its size, melting ice and 'causing dew to fall
from a clear sky'.[6]

A passage of Gregory of Nazanzus sounds for a
moment as though he envisages a Copernican universe,
when he describes us finding ourselves 'as lesser lights
circling round the great light',[7] but he does not mean
this. 'One does not blame the sun for its movement,'
he writes to Gregory of Nyssa, 'nor the planets for their
wandering.'[8] Gregory's universe is firmly Aristotelian.

The moon undergoes changes in periods of seven days,
writes Clement of Alexandria. In one seven-day period

---

[1] *Hex.*, iii.7.69ab.
[2] *in Hex.*, P.G., 44.113b–117c.
[3] ibid., 76d–77a.   [4] *ad. Autol.*, i.5.
[5] *Cat.*, xviii.3.
[6] *Hex.*, vi.9.137cd; 140ab; vi.10.141a.
[7] *Orat.*, xviii.40.   [8] *Ep.*, 81.

it is a half moon; in the second week it is full; in the third it wanes to half; in the fourth it disappears.[1] To this Basil adds that the moon marks one year by making twelve circuits to its course.[2]

Gregory of Nyssa maintains that the moon is a source of light, not merely a reflector of light, though he admits that its light is feeble.[3] Basil agrees with this, and says that when the moon wanes, its body is not consumed but is deprived of the light which envelops it, giving an illusion of diminution. He advances as proof the fact that on a clear night the full circle of the moon is faintly visible when only a semi-circle is illuminated. He dismisses the notion that the moon has only borrowed light.[4] The light of the moon gives an indication of its size. Wherever you stand on earth, the rays of the moon run parallel, whereas a small light sends out rays pointing in all directions.[5] Despite his dismissal of astronomy as useless,[6] Basil admits the influence of the moon upon mundane affairs. It can, for example, be used to forecast weather 'according to observations made by those who have leisure for such researches'. The state of the atmosphere around the earth changes with the phases of the moon. Thinner atmosphere 'towards the third day', with a brightly shining moon, indicates fine weather to some. Thickness of atmosphere and a red moon in its crescent phase presage violent southerly winds.[7] The moon also affects the constitution of animals, which grow and dwindle in sympathy with it. Fresh meat rapidly turns bad under the moon's influence. Rough seas follow a full moon,

[1] *Strom.*, vi.16.143.2, 3; cf. Theophilus of Ant., *ad Autol.*, i.13; ii.16; Theodoret, *de prov.*, i., *P.G.*, 83.569c.

[2] *Hex.*, vi.8.137b.

[3] *in Hex.*, *P.G.*, 44.117b.

[4] *Hex.*, vi.3.121d; 124ac.

[5] *Hex.*, vi.10.145ab.

[6] *Hex.*, ix.1.189a.

[7] *Hex.*, vi.4.125c.

and ocean tides are affected, as though the moon were inhaling and exhaling.[1]

On the age of the earth, Origen taunts Celsus with allowing himself to be forced into a position in which he argues that the world is comparatively recent in origin, not yet ten thousand years old,[2] and Theophilus of Antioch ridicules pagan chronology: Apollonius the Egyptian says that the world is 153,075 years old, writes Theophilus, which conflicts with the biblical evidence.[3] The discovery of fish high in the precipices of the mountains of Libanus, 'as though pickled and dried and preserved to this day', is evidence for Eusebius of the depth of the flood rather than the age of the earth.[4]

Belief that the earth would end in a conflagration is widespread, deriving in part from Jewish-Christian apocalyptic doctrine and in part from Platonic and Stoic sources. Origen agrees with Plato's words about the earth being purified by blood and fire, and accepts the Stoic idea of the final conflagration while denying that of the cosmic rebirth which would follow it. The fire will be for discipline, not for destruction. He admits an analogy between the Stoic rebirth after *ecpyrosis* and the Christian doctrine of resurrection.[5] Before Origen, pseudo-Clement had pictured the earth melting like lead in the fire,[6] and Hermas had seen it being destroyed by fire and blood.[7]

On the structure of the universe Athenagoras notes simply that the earth is spherical in shape and is confined within the circles of heaven.[8] The earth is central

---

[1] *Hex.*, vi.10.144ab.   [2] *c. Cels.*, i.20.

[3] *ad Autol.*, iii.16. Theophilus also ridicules those who believe the world to be spherical in shape, *ad Autol.*, ii.30–2.

[4] Armenian *Chronicle*, *G.C.S.*, V, p. 41.

[5] *c. Cels.*, iv.20; iv.77; v.15; v.20.

[6] *Ep.*, ii.16.3.

[7] *Pastor*, i.4.3.

[8] *Suppl.*, viii, xvi.

to the system as the hub of a wheel is to its circumference, writes Cyril of Jerusalem.[1] Gregory of Nyssa sees the motion of the system holding it together; the earth is composed of heavy, motionless substances, and is kept in position by the rapid revolutions of the spheres encircling it, compressing the compact body of the earth.[2] The orbital motion of the stars suggests to Basil that they are constituted differently from other bodies. Simple bodies, he says, move in rectilinear fashion, light bodies moving upwards and heavy bodies downwards. But bodies which move differently, round a circumference as the stars do, must therefore be differently constituted.[3] Unlike Eusebius, who sees no difficulty here,[4] he rejects the idea of the air forming a couch which supports the mass of the earth, and argues that the air would be forced apart by the weight of the earth. Similarly, the earth would sink if it were supported by water, even supposing that it could be ascertained what supported the water.[5] The hypothesis that another body supports the earth equally demands an answer to the question, what supports the other body? The matter is beyond our understanding, Basil concludes; the earth is in the hand of God.[6] It is plain to Basil, however, that the earth is motionless, and he subscribes to the opinion of 'natural philosophers' that the earth, being central to the universe, must remain immobile in order to preserve the balance of the whole.[7] The earth is itself balanced, says Novatian, lest its mass, lying askew, should fall into ruins.[8]

Basil's disclaimer early in the *Hexaemeron* that he is competent to say anything about the constitution of the

---

[1] *Cat.*, vi.3.   [2] *de hom. opif.*, i.1.3.
[3] *Hex.*, i.11.25ab.
[4] *Prae. Evang.*, vii.10.314b.
[5] *Hex.*, i.8.21bc; cf. Aristotle, *de coelo*, ii.13.294ab.
[6] *Hex.*, i.9.21c, 24b.   [7] *Hex.*, i.10.24b.
[8] *de Trin.*, iii.

heavens other than that they are 'of a light substance, neither solid nor thick', is hardly maintained by his subsequent speculations on the subject.[1] A distinction must be made, he argues, between the firmament and the heavens. The distinction had not always been made: for Tatian the term 'heavens' represented a finite, limited area beyond which lay 'the superior worlds which are not subject to seasons or disease',[2] while for Theophilus of Antioch it is the firmament which is visible to us and the heavens invisible beyond it, the firmament retaining half the water above it to provide rain and dew.[3] Basil, asserting the distinction, ridicules what he calls the artificial linear construction of the heavens as envisaged by Plato and Aristotle. It is no stranger, he claims, to think of two heavens than of seven circles in which the planets move.[4] The word 'firmament' suggests to Basil something stronger than the heavens which had been created previously. The firmament can be observed to be spherical: how then can it hold water, as it is said to do at Genesis i.7? From our terrestrial viewpoint its under surface appears to be concave, but it does not follow that its upper surface must be so.[5] The human eye cannot take in the depth from the concave inner circumference to the more distant convex outer surface.[6] Gregory of Nyssa is also troubled by the question of water retained above the firmament. Why is the water not thrown off by the rotation of the heavens about the pole?[7] Possibly because the upper side of the firmament is pitted into valleys analogous to those on earth, but Gregory scorns opponents who may 'think up some kind of cups in the spheres' to hold the water.[8] The term 'firmament' again suggests to Basil that it is composed of some

---

[1] *Hex.*, i.7.20c; 21ab.
[2] *Orat. ad Graec.*, xx.
[3] *ad Autol.*, ii.13.
[4] *Hex.*, iii.3.56d; 57b.
[5] *Hex.*, iii.3.60a; 4.60b.
[6] *Ep.*, 233.
[7] *in Hex.*, *P.G.*, 44.66d.
[8] ibid., 89a-c.

resistant matter such as condensed air. The fact that it
is associated with water need not lead us to suppose
that it is composed of frozen water, nor anything like
crystal, formed by some unusual congealing of water.
Crystal is a brilliant stone of pure transparency, resistant to erosion by water and not split by faults, and
almost as transparent as air. The firmament, however, must be composed of the four elements, singly or
in combination.[1] It filters upwards the lightest particles
of liquid, and downwards the heaviest.[2] Gregory of
Nyssa is not so confident. It might be composed of any
of the four elements, or of a fifth, but in any case it is not
solid, nor is it capable of being apprehended by the
senses, nor of being destroyed by fire.[3] Chrysostom
asserts man's total ignorance of the composition of the
heavens: scripture, not reason, tells us that it is a vault
covering the whole earth, but we have no idea whether
it is composed of ice or condensed cloud or compacted
air.[4] Gregory is not entirely satisfied that Basil has
covered the matter adequately—his *Hexaemeron* was,
after all, addressed to a mixed audience. There are, says
Gregory, three heavens: first, the region of denser
atmosphere which is used by the birds which fly highest;
secondly, the region of the planets; thirdly, that of the
firmament, and what Paul in II Corinthians xii calls
'the third heaven'.[5] Theodoret is content to write
simply that the heavens do not melt under the heat of
the sun, moon and stars, but are of a nature resistant to
heat.[6]

Finally, it must be noted that beneath the surface of
the earth lay the abyss or pit, akin to the Hebrew *Sheol*,

[1] *Hex.*, iii.4.60c; 61a-c.

[2] *Hex.*, iii.7.68c.

[3] *in Hex.*, *P.G.*, 44.80cd.

[4] *de incomp.*, ii, *P.G.*, 48.717d; *Comm. in Rom.*, xxviii (Rom. xv.13);
cf. Irenaeus, *adv. haer.*, ii.28.2; Eusebius, *Prae. Evang.* vii.10.314b.

[5] *in Hex.*, *P.G.*, 44.121a-c.

[6] *de prov.*, i., *P.G.*, 83.564ab.

a place, says Novatian, whither the souls of the just and the unjust are taken, conscious of the anticipated dooms of judgment to come.[1] Theophilus of Antioch describes God as fixing the confines of the depths and setting the earth above the water,[2] and Origen defines the term 'universe' to include 'everything which is above the heavens or in the heavens or upon the earth or in those places which are called the lower regions'.[3] Even the abyss, says Basil, contributes to the praise which the whole universe offers to God.[4]

Meteorology

Exhalations which arise from the earth and from marshes gather into mists and cloudy masses, writes Clement of Alexandria.[5] Gregory of Nyssa and Basil add further detail: it is warmth that causes these vapours to gather, and in colder areas, such as those subject to North winds, there is less evaporation.[6] Where vapours are drawn up from moist ground by the sun, the substance of air is made visible,[7] the moisture preventing the aether from consuming everything, being in its turn transformed by the sun into vapour and consumed.[8] Not quite consistently, Basil says elsewhere that in winter the air grows cold and vapours arise from the earth to cause rain and snow.[9] The moisture drawn from the earth becomes rain through compression. Moisture, writes Basil, collects in the sky in clouds, condenses and falls as rain.[10] Gregory of Nyssa

---

[1] de Trin., 1.   [2] ad Autol., i.6.7.
[3] de princ., ii.9.3.   [4] Hex., iii.9.76c.
[5] Strom., ii.20.115.3.
[6] Greg. Nyssa, in Hex., P.G., 44.93b–d; 100b; cf. de hom. opif., xiii.13.
[7] Basil, Hex., i.7.20b; cf. Eusebius' note on the effect of sun and moon on the atmosphere, Prae. Evang., iii.11.109a.
[8] Hex., iii.7.69b.
[9] Hex., vi.8.136a.
[10] Hex., iii.8.73a; cf. Plato, Timaeus, 49c; Arist., Meteor., i.9.346b.

says that the nature of cloud is a sort of vapour, light and of great subtlety, and when forced together by compression falls through the air as drops of rain.[1] Basil again adds details reminiscent of Aristotle: moisture evaporates in the air and becomes cold in the upper air when it passes beyond the rays of the sun, after which it returns as rain.[2] It is not, however, simply low temperature which gives rise to snow. When moisture is buffeted by winds it turns to froth, becomes frozen, and falls as snow.[3] Gregory of Nyssa traces two independent cycles of events: water on the surface of the earth evaporates, rises and in the upper regions of the atmosphere is dried by the heat of the sun, returning to earth as a kind of ash analogous to the black soot deposited by burning oil in a lamp. On reaching the colder region of the earth's surface this is transformed back into water. Thus, Gregory concludes, the quantity of water remains constant. The dry particles are hard to see except in a ray of sunshine, in which they can be observed moving earthwards.[4] There is a second cycle more like Basil's account of the matter, which Gregory does not succeed wholly in correlating with the first: moisture evaporates, rises, and is compressed to form a cloud which falls back to earth as rain.[5] Gregory seems not to envisage rain water as soaking into the earth, but as being used simply by plants for purposes of nourishment. The drying of the vapour by the sun's rays consumes part of it, and there is some replenishment from subterranean sources, water rising from below through veins and faults in the rock.[6] Gregory

---

[1] *c. Eunom.*, iii.2; so Novatian, *de spect.*, ix; Theophilus of Ant., *ad Autol.*, i.6; Basil, *Hex.*, vi.4.125b; *Ep.*, 38; Cyril of Jerus., *Cat.*, ix.9; Theodoret, *de prov.*, i, *P.G.*, 83.569d, 577b.

[2] *Hex.*, iv.6.43a; cf. Arist., *Meteor.*, i.3.340a.

[3] *Hex.*, iii.8.73a; cf. Ps.-Arist., *de Mundo*, iv.394a.

[4] *in Hex.*, *P.G.*, 44.113a. For the analogy of the deposit on a lamp, 97b, 98c, 105a.

[5] ibid., 93d–96a.   [6] ibid., 109d.

also suggests that the atmosphere further from the surface of the earth is more rarified, his evidence for this being that high mountain peaks above cloud level are devoid of birds and animals that require air.[1] In Nemesius' view, the process by which one element can change into another, e.g. water into vapour, is change in one of its qualities. Water, by exchanging cold for heat, is transformed into air.[2]

It is worth noting in parenthesis at this point a fine descriptive passage in a letter of Gregory of Nyssa to Ablabius:

Suddenly the clouds gathered thick, and there was a change from clear sky to deep gloom. Then a chilly breeze blowing through the clouds brought drizzle with it and made us very damp, threatening such rain as had never been known. To our left there were continuous claps of thunder alternating with vivid flashes of lightning . . . and all the mountains in front, behind and to either side were enveloped in cloud.

Yet still the heavy rain did not fall. 'There was a little drizzle, not unpleasant but just enough to moisten the air. Shortly before we reached home, however, the cloud over our heads condensed into a heavier shower.'[3] Gregory was not always so fortunate. In another letter he describes a visit to his opponent Helladius, involving a journey of fifteen miles on horseback over rough country: 'A storm cloud, gathered into a mass in the clear air by an eddy of wind, drenched us to the skin with torrents of rain, for owing to the sultry atmosphere we had made no preparations against rain.'[4]

There is little distinction made between rain and dew. Theophilus of Antioch describes dew as being stored with the rain above the firmament,[5] and Basil

---

[1] ibid., 96c.   [2] *de nat. hom.*, v.24.
[3] *Ep.*, 3.   [4] *Ep.*, 18.
[5] *ad Autol.*, ii.13; cf. i.6.

observes without comment that dew appears to fall
from a clear sky.[1] Gregory of Nazianzus twice notes the
rapid dispersal of dew by morning sun.[2]

The Cappadocians appear to have suffered from
violent rain storms. A letter to Theodosius, possibly by
Basil, asks for a bridge over the river Halys. Heavy snow
in the marsh lands had resulted in serious flooding. Before
the snow could freeze, a warm breeze brought southerly
rain, swelling the tributaries of the Halys to cause such
flooding that transport of goods for sale over the river
was halted and the grass and plough land ruined.[3]
Gregory of Nazianzus addresses his father's congregation on the occasion of the ruin of their crops by storms
of rain and hail.[4] In the spring of 371 Basil apologises
to Eusebius of Samosata for not having written to
him earlier: he could not find a carrier to take the
letter, since his people so shuddered at the winter that
they could not bring themselves to set foot out of doors.
Indeed, says Basil, we have been overwhelmed with
such a mass of snow that for two months we have been
lurking in our burrows, buried with our houses.[5] To
Libanius he writes: 'I write this letter under a blanket
of snow. Our houses are graves until the Spring brings
us to life again like the plants.'[6] Gregory of Nyssa
describes ice forming inside the cottages after rain had
come in, and then moisture spreading over the frozen
surface and forming a fresh coat of ice.[7] The remark in
a letter attributed to Basil, that 'our land is subject to
frosts', reads like an understatement.[8] We may hope
that Basil, who knew Origen's work well, drew comfort

[1] *Hex.*, vi.10.141a.   [2] *Orat.*, vii.19; xviii.26.

[3] Basil, *Ep.*, 365. cf. Theodoret on winters when flooding for-
bids the passage of man and beast alike, *de prov.*, P.G., 83.573b.

[4] *Orat.*, xvi.   [5] *Ep.*, 48.

[6] *Ep.*, 350.   [7] *Ep.*, 9.

[8] *Ep.*, 365. Chrysostom describes the Cappadocian shepherds
remaining buried for three days under snow, *Comm. in Rom.*, xxix
(Rom. xv.24).

from Origen's assurance that we do not have unvaryingly productive or unproductive seasons, nor yet periods of continuous rain or drought.[1]

Of thunder, Theophilus of Antioch says that it is preceded by lightning to warn us and save us from too great fear.[2] Basil finely compares the shock of the news of the death of Athanasius with the shock of deafness caused by a loud clap of thunder.[3] Equally good is the observation of Gregory of Nazianzus of a man suddenly left in the dark by a flash of lightning.[4] Gregory appears to have been pleased with his remark in one oration that the truth escapes us before we have grasped it as does a lightning flash, for he repeats it on a later occasion.[5] He will not commit himself to an explanation of the phenomena of thunder and lightning, and simply asks whether lightning could be caused by strong pressure of air within a cloud, and thunder by violent release of pressure.[6] Basil's explanation is that the cause is agitation of air compressed in the cavities of the clouds.[7]

It is moisture in the atmosphere that causes a rainbow.[8] The bow is formed when moisture is pressed together, creating an opaque mass. Light from the sun strikes this mass and reproduces on it a patch of light similar in shape to the sun itself, that is, circular. The light is then thrown back, for light is reflected from a surface that is wet and shiny. Since the sun is circular the light appears on the moist air as circular in shape. Basil's account of the colours of the rainbow shows him to be imperfectly acquainted with the spectrum. The rainbow, he says, appears to be composed of a single

---

[1] c. Cels., iv.64. [2] ad Autol., i.6.
[3] Ep., 29; cf. Greg. Naz., Orat., xli.6.
[4] Orat., ii.74. [5] ibid., xxxviii.7; xlv.3.
[6] ibid., xxviii.28.
[7] Hex., iii.4.61a; cf. Comm. in Psalm., xxviii.1.118a.
[8] Basil, Hex., vi.4.125c. The rainbow forecasts rain to follow.

c

band of colour and yet is actually of many colours mingled imperceptibly. It is hard to find the point where the blue-green merges into yellow, or yellow into purple, or purple into amber, or to see how far the red and the green extend,[1] which is what Clement of Alexandria had said more simply, that it is impossible to depict a rainbow in paint.[2]

Botany and horticulture

Here we find evidence not only of study of botanical material in written sources, but possibly also of careful observation. Basil claims that a single plant can occupy one's whole attention, indicating as an example a corn stem encircled by joints, so that the ligatures allow it to support the weight of the ears when they are ripe and bend earthwards. This, he says, is the function of the ligatures, since the corn stem is hollow throughout and needs reinforcement. The grain is deposited in a container to protect it from the birds, and the spikes of the corn protect it from small animals.[3] He distinguishes wheat from black wheat: the blackness indicates disease caused by heat, not a separate variety. Tares and other bastard growths which mix with food crops are not wheat at all, but a different species.[4] Basil's attempt at classifying trees in *Hexaemeron* v.7 is characteristic of his confusion when he attempts classification. Recognising the difficulty of the matter he suggests various criteria: depth of root; single stemmed or multiple; the relationship between spread of branch and spread of root; difference of bark, smooth or wrinkled. The classification degenerates into a random list of differences between one variety of tree and another. There are wide variations, he says, within a single type of fruit tree. He observes the difference between the resin of the mastich and the sap of the balsam; between the juices of the vine and the olive, the apple, fig, palm, wormwood and terebinth. After apologising for having become 'lost in digressions through an insatiable desire to contemplate everything', Basil makes a last attempt at classification: there are evergreen and deciduous trees, the former being sub-divided into those with weak and strong foliage, the pine and the olive in effect losing their foliage, the palm keeping it.[1] We may feel that Basil is on safer ground when drawing attention to similarities than when attempting differentiation. The elm, he says, like the willow and the black and white poplars, does not appear to bear fruit, but close inspection shows that in fact a seed is formed under the leaf. A tree of this kind is called μισχός.[2] Like Origen, Basil is disturbed by the apparent suggestion at Genesis i.11 that the seed comes from the green shoots of a plant, and for this botanical reason corrects the text of Genesis to read, *Let the earth bring forth the green shoots and the seed*.[3] He notes that some plants do not appear to carry seeds, such as the reed, mint, crocus, garlic and sedge. Many plants, however, carry their seminal force in their root and stem.[4] The reed, he writes, after its annual growth, produces a bud on its root, which takes the place of a seed.[5] The process of germination is described by Basil as follows, and applies, he says, to all growth, whether of cereals, seeds in pods, garden vegetables or scrub. The seed falls into

[1] *Hex.*, v.7.107bc; 112a; 113a-c; 116b. There are suggestions throughout the passage that it rests upon Theophrastus, *Hist. plant.*, i.4.1; i.5.2; i.6.4; i.8; i.9.3; and *de caus. plant.*, i.13.

[2] *Hex.*, v.6.105c; 108a. cf. Theophrastus, *Hist plant.*, iii.1.2; iii.3.4.; iii.7.3, whose details are in some respects similar to those of Basil, though it can hardly be claimed that Basil is copying directly at this point.

[3] Origen, *Hom. in Gen.*, *P.G.*, 12.92c; Basil, *Hex.*, v.2.96b.

[4] *Hex.*, v.2.97a.

[5] Possibly a mis-reading of Theophrastus, *Hist. plant.*, ii.2.1, where a sentence concerning root growth follows immediately upon one concerning reeds.

the soil and becomes soft and porous, enabling it to 'take hold of the soil' and absorb the elements of the soil appropriate to it. Minute particles of soil pass into the seed through the pores and cause it to increase in size by pushing out roots and stretching upwards, putting out as many stems as roots. The nourishment from the earth passes through the whole plant.[1]

It is characteristic of Clement of Alexandria's interest in the practical aspect of arboriculture that he should correct without comment Paul's metaphor in Romans xi of a wild olive branch being grafted on to a culti- vated stock. He simply reverses Paul's process, making greater sense botanically and nonsense metaphorically.[2] Other fathers show greater reverence for the letter of the Pauline text than for botanical consistency. Cyril of Jerusalem[3] and Chrysostom[4] follow Paul in describing the convert grafted from the wild olive into the culti- vated. Gregory of Nazianzus does so twice.[5] Irenaeus not only follows but expands and develops the idea.[6] Clement is willing to concede that a convert can be transplanted from poor soil to good soil, after which his fruitfulness increases,[7] but not that a bad branch is grafted on to a good stock. The reason for grafting on to a wild stock, he says, is that wild trees attract more nourishment on account of their being unable to ripen, therefore the graft receives more nourishment than it would ordinarily have received.[8] On the practice of grafting, Clement says that there are four methods: the first, in which the graft must be fitted between the wood and the bark; the second, in which the wood is cut and the cultivated growth is inserted into the cut; the third,

---

[1] *Hex.*, v.3.100cd.

[2] *Strom.*, vi.15.118.1, 'The grafted olive receives more nourish- ment from the fact of its having been grafted into a wild one.'

[3] *Cat.*, 1.4.   [4] *Comm. in Rom.*, xix.

[5] *Orat.*, vii.3; xviii.11.   [6] *adv. haer.*, v.10.1, 2.

[7] *Strom.*, vi.2.4.   [8] ibid., vi.15.117f.

in which the graft and the stock are bound together after stripping off each sucker with a sharp pruning knife till the pith is laid bare without being wounded; the fourth type is called budding, in which an eye is cut out of a cultivated trunk, a circle of bark round it being included. Then the trunk which is to receive the graft is stripped of bark over an area equal to that of the graft, and the latter is inserted, tied and daubed with clay, the eye itself being kept uninjured and unstained.[1] Gregory of Nyssa also describes the last method, the removing of a shoot 'cut off with some bark for a base', which is then fitted into an incision made in the other tree.[2] Clement writes approvingly of the Deuteronomic injunctions concerning the care of trees: cultivated species are not to be felled; young trees are to be cared for continuously during their first three years, their superfluous growth being cut off so that they do not become overweighted, nor exhausted through wasting their nourishment. There is to be digging around their roots to remove suckers. Fruit must not be picked from immature trees.[3] Origen says that in pruning, the old growth must be cut right back to a bud in order to encourage fresh growth.[4] The pruning hook, writes Clement, though used primarily for pruning, is also used for separating vine twigs that have become entangled, and for cutting the thorns that grow along with the vines.[5] If one wants to gather clusters from a vine, one must lop, dig and bind, for which the pruning knife and the pick axe are used.[6] The vine that is not pruned grows to wood.[7] Basil gives a different reason for pruning: vine leaves have to be cut back to increase the plant's resistance to injury and to expose the fruit

---

[1] ibid., vi.15.119.1–4.   [2] in Hex., P.G., 44.64.b.
[3] Strom., ii.18.95.1f.
[4] Comm. in Cant., iv.14 (Cant. ii.10–13).
[5] Strom., vi.8.65.5.   [6] ibid., i.9.43.1.
[7] Paed., i.8.66.4.

to the sun.[1] Cuttings, he says, should be taken from
shoots springing from the root of a plant.[2] Defects in
fruit can be corrected by proper treatment of a tree:
the fruit of the pomegranate and the bitter almond can
be rendered sweeter if their bark is pierced a little way
above the root and a sticky wedge of pine is driven into
the incision to penetrate as far as the central core of the
tree.[3]

Clement of Alexandria perhaps speaks with the voice
of experience when he demands whether the gardener
is to abandon gardening simply because weeds spring
up among his vegetables.[4] Basil too may be casting his
mind back to the days when he cultivated the ground
about his hermitage, when he writes of an over-enthusi-
astic theologian: 'I like to compare Dionysius with a
gardener who, in trying to correct the bent of a young
plant, miscalculates the counter-strain and bends the
stem too far the other way.'[5] If Basil sees his Cappadocian landscapes almost with a Romantic eye (we
shall notice his description in more detail at a later
point),[6] Clement writes almost with the touch of a
second-century Bacon when he describes his *Stromata* as
being laid out not like a garden, planted in regular order
for the delight of the eye, but rather like a shady and
natural hillside, where the gardener will conceal fruit
trees among the rest to hide them from pilferers and
which he will use as a nursery from which to transplant
and take cuttings for a formal garden.[7] We may also
notice at this point the graceful letter of Basil to the
pagan Libanius, a letter whose attribution to Basil has
been questioned, in which he says that though Libanius'

[1] *Hex.*, v.8.112d.   [2] *Hex.*, v.6.108a.
[3] *Hex.*, v.7.109d.   [4] *Strom.*, vii.16.91.6.
[5] *Ep.*, 9; Greg. Naz., *Orat.*, xlv.12, for a similar idea in a different
context.
[6] See below, p. 87.
[7] *Strom.*, vii.18.111.1.

letters are prickly, those who love roses are not deterred
by the thorns.[1]

Zoology

In this branch of science perhaps more than any other
the Greek fathers show themselves to be unscientific,
expressing ideas which are a curious mixture of fact and
fancy. And yet they are not wholly uncritical. Mythi-
cal creatures, some of which would provide excellent
material in support of doctrinal and moral points, are
treated by some writers with a reserve which suggests
their willingness to remain loyal to the facts of nature so
far as they could ascertain them. Clement of Rome, at
the turn of the first century A.D., is indeed willing to
accept the phoenix legend at its face value, and wel-
comes it as evidence of resurrection in the natural world,
giving a full account of the creature;[2] and Cyril of
Jerusalem in the fourth century says that we should not
disbelieve the phoenix story, since wonderful things
happen in the natural world.[3] But Origen is more
cautious and says that if the legend be true, it is possible
that the sequence of events related of the phoenix may
occur in consequence of some provision of nature.[4] Of
the goat stag Origen says bluntly that it cannot exist,
and that the griffon is not recorded to have been cap-
tured by man.[5] Gregory of Nyssa dismisses the goat stag
as an imaginary combination of two animals,[6] and
Gregory of Nazianzus says simply that it is an invention.[7]
Both, however, mention the salamander without ad-
verse comment.[8] The basilisk, described by Origen as an
object of pagan worship,[9] is again treated less critically

[1] *Ep.*, 342.   [2] *ad Cor.*, xxv.1–4.
[3] *Cat.*, xviii.8.   [4] *c. Cels.*, iv.98.
[5] *de princ.*, iv.1.17.   [6] *Ep.*, 15.
[7] *Orat.*, xxxi.6.
[8] Greg. Nyssa, *c. Eunom.*, i.27; viii.3; Greg. Naz., *Orat.* xlii.21.
[9] *c. Cels.*, iv.54.

by Cyril of Jerusalem, who speaks of its gaze being its means of defence.[1] Athenagoras, appearing to think that belief in legendary creatures calls for some word of explanation, says that 'we are well aware that some beasts have human forms, or have a nature compounded of men and beasts'.[2] It is in this setting of something less than complete credulity that we should see their attempts to describe and explain more familiar creatures.

Some creatures appear to attract legend. The viper, for example, is said to be eaten by deer when they are sick;[3] to mate with the eel, attracting it by whistling;[4] to be eaten by the tortoise, marjoram being consumed as an antidote to the poison;[5] to eat its own mother.[6] Bats are said by Basil to keep contact during flight by a kind of chain, one suspended from the other.[7] The bear, according to Clement of Alexandria, gives birth to a shapeless lump of flesh and licks it into shape.[8] Clement's brief note that oil is dangerous to bees[9] is expanded by Basil, who says that the oil clogs the pores and causes death, and that if the dead bee is dipped in vinegar it recovers.[10] In the same passage Basil says that bees have no respiration or lung, but breathe with their whole body.[11] According to Cyril of Jerusalem, bees can be drowned in water and yet revive, and young bees are fashioned out of worms, a metamorphosis which he regards as miraculous, analogous to the resurrection of the phoenix.[12] Rather similarly Origen describes the generating of bees from the body of an ox, in accordance with what he calls the established laws regulating

[1] *Cat.*, ix.14.   [2] *de. res. mort.*, vii.
[3] Tatian, *Orat. ad Graec.*, xviii; cf. Origen, *c. Cels.*, ii.48.
[4] Basil, *Hex.*, vii.5.160c.   [5] ibid., ix.3.193a.
[6] ibid., ix.5.200a.   [7] ibid., vii.7.181a.
[8] *Strom.*, vi.6.50.3.   [9] *Paed.*, ii.8.
[10] *Hex.*, viii.7.184a.
[11] This group of ideas may be associated with Aristotle's remarks about the absence of inhalation in insects, *Hist. An.*, i.1.487a.
[12] *Cat.*, xviii.8.

the metamorphosis of bodies.[1] To the assertion of Celsus
that snakes and eagles can perform sorcery, being
acquainted with cures for diseases and with 'the virtues
of certain stones which help to preserve their young',
Origen admits the fact but dismisses the idea of sorcery:
it is 'either experience or some natural power of apprehension' which prompts eagles to carry to their nest the
eagle stone to protect their young.[2] Basil reflects a belief
widespread in antiquity that the earth produced life
when he says that eels are born of mud, with no eggs or
other means of reproduction.[3] The legend approved by
Celsus that elephants make and keep oaths is dismissed
as nonsense by Origen.[4] Of the hare, Barnabas writes,
'the hare every year multiplies the places of its conception, the number of such passages corresponding to
the years it has lived'.[5] Clement of Alexandria repeats
the wording of Barnabas in explanation of Deuteronomy
xiv.7, but then says that the hare has two passages to the
womb, a duplication of organs which leads to indiscri-
minate coition.[6] Novatian implies the sexual deformity
of the hare.[7] In the same chapters, Barnabas and
Clement repeat the common legend that the hyaena
changes its sex yearly, Clement going on to describe the
hyaena as possessing a protuberance of flesh beneath
the tail, which has no function since it leads neither to
womb nor intestine and contains only a useless concavity. The halcyon, according to Basil, is a sea bird
which hatches its eggs on the shore. The eggs hatch in
midwinter when the sea is rough, but the wind and sea
are calm during the seven days in which the bird
broods. Seven more days see the growth of the young.[8]
Clement of Alexandria repeats a Libyan legend that if
a scorpion fails to sting its victim, it fetches others to

[1] *c. Cels.*, iv.57.   [2] ibid., iv.86.
[3] *Hex.*, ix.2.192a.   [4] *c. Cels.*, iv.88.
[5] *Ep.*, x.6.   [6] *Paed.*, ii.10.
[7] *de cib. jud.*, iii.   [8] *Hex.*, viii.5.177ab.

help.[1] Origen appears to accept the idea that a snake
can be generated out of a dead man, 'growing, as the
multitude affirm, out of the marrow of the back'.[2] If a
swallow's eyes are put out, says Basil, nature restores
their sight.[3]

It is easy to dismiss these fairy tales with a smile and
to contrast them with passages in which the fathers give
zoological information which is less out of keeping with
a twentieth-century view of scientific fact; as though
they had picked up the legends from old wives and the
facts from scientific text books, and should have distinguished more critically between reliable and unreliable sources. But they wrote in the manner of the
age in which they lived. Even writers such as Pliny,
Aelian and Oppian, whose aim was more specifically
to collect and disseminate information about the natural
world, present their readers with the same mixture of
fact and fancy, and by no means all the fathers knew
even such writers as these at first hand. It is likely that
most of their information would have been obtained
from a manual or *epitome* of natural history, in which
the conclusions of Aristotle and Theophrastus and Galen
would appear side by side with folklore and legend, and
most of them would lack the detailed knowledge which
would enable them to sift fact from fancy. In any case,
says Cyril of Jerusalem, marvellous things happen in
the natural world.[4] It is worth noting that the Alexandrian Origen often shows a more critical spirit towards legendary creatures and occurrences than is
shown by the reputedly more rationalistic Antiocenes.

Some patristic observations have a modern ring about
them, as Clement of Alexandria's note that eggs may be
hatched artificially if subjected to the right temperature, or his account of fowls being fattened in darkness

---

[1] *Strom.*, i.21.143.3.   [2] *c. Cels.*, iv.57.
[3] *Hex.*, viii.2.169b.
[4] *Cat.*, xviii.8.

and fed for killing.[1] His description of the nightingale's change of note in winter may or may not be correct in fact, but it has the characteristic of not avoiding the issue by invoking the wonders of nature; it is an attempt at a real explanation. The bird changes its colour and its song together, he writes, though this must not be seen as a change in its nature, as a change of sex would be. The feathers fade with the onset of winter, and at the same time the voice is affected by the cold. In consequence of the outer skin being thickened by the colder air around it, the passages of the throat become constricted and press hard on the breath, which, being confined, produces a stifled sound. When the breathing is relaxed in spring, it is carried through the dilated passages, and the bird no longer makes a dying melody but utters a shrill note.[2] Basil explains the varied lengths of animals' necks in relation to their feeding habits: the bear and the lion are carnivorous and therefore do not need long necks to stretch for their food; the camel, being herbivorous, has a suitably long neck; the elephant is herbivorous, with a trunk which compensates for its shortness of neck.[3] Apart from explanations of this kind, there are unexplained observations of zoological phenomena which, whether accurate or not, have the right ring to them. They are not merely fanciful. Fish, says Basil, are markedly similar to birds. There is similarity between fins and wings ('one swimming through the water, the other in the air'[4]) and in the way in which fish and birds alike steer themselves by their tails.[5] Fish breathe, he says, by dilation and contraction of the gills, which fill with water and then expel it, a process which takes the place of respiration.[6] Theophilus

---

[1] *Strom.*, vii.4.26.3; *Protrept.*, xi.113.3. For ancient references see the note in loc. by Père Claude Mondésert, S.J., in *Sources chrétiennes*, ii.2 (Paris 1949).   [2] *Paed.*, ii.10.

[3] *Hex.*, ix.5.200c.   [4] *Ep.*, 188.

[5] *Hex.*, viii.2.169a.   [6] *Hex.*, vii.1.149b.

describes a bird eating seed and leaving the seed in
its droppings, and the seed, 'which has passed through
so great heat', germinates.[1] Basil, despite his fanciful
account of bats linked in flight by a kind of chain, can
describe a bat with some precision: it is both quadruped
and winged, unique in possessing teeth, viviparous, fly-
ing not on feathered wings but on membranes of skin.[2]
Writing of sheep, he says that a lamb and ewe recognise
each other in a flock 'not by colour or voice or even
smell, as far as we can judge, but by some sense more
subtle than our intelligence'.[3]

The instances of astronomical, meteorological, botanical and zoological observation which have been cited
in the foregoing pages represent only a small proportion
of the passages in which the Greek fathers mention
natural objects or processes. The passages selected for
inclusion here have been those in which a clear point
is made about the phenomenon in question. It must be
emphasised again that the writers were not discussing
the natural world for its own sake and in a spirit of
detached scientific enquiry. Nature was of great importance to the fathers, but almost always for some
reason other than the pursuit of scientific knowledge.
Perhaps the nearest we come to the pursuit of knowledge for its own sake is what H.-I. Marrou calls the
'pure *curiositas*' of Clement of Alexandria;[4] but we are
not very near even at this point, for Clement's mind is
too wayward and his erudition, though considerable,
too fragmentary. The most careful and probably the
most original observations of the natural world are
made by Nemesius,[5] but he pursues scientific matters
for their moral and theological bearing. This is true of

[1] *ad Autol.*, i.13.   [2] *Hex.*, viii.3.172a.
[3] *Hex.*, ix.4.197a.
[4] *Paedagogos:* Texte, Introd. et Notes, H.-I. Marrou et M. Harl
(Sources chrétiennes 70, Paris 1960), p. 77.
[5] See Ch. 2 for an account of Nemesius, *On The Nature of Man.*

the fathers as a whole, and at once reveals that they are spiritually akin to Plato rather than to Aristotle.

The Greek sources underlying the fathers' work are almost wholly literary and philosophical rather than scientific. Theophilus of Antioch, for example, though himself used as a source by others, notably Basil, reveals familiarity with the Greek historians and tragedians and perhaps with Plato, but otherwise worked from manuals and florilegia.[1] Clement of Alexandria's observations of nature have parallels in Pliny, Solinus, Pollux, Aulus Gellius, Plutarch, Athenaeus and Aelian, but here, as in his references to Greek dramatists, poets and historians, it is probable that he used an intermediary source.[2] Origen appears to have had some knowledge of geometry, astronomy and medicine, and knew the work of Aristotle at first hand, but more probably the philosophical work rather than the scientific.[3] With Basil we are moving in a more genuinely scientific sphere, though Basil's once high reputation as a scientific writer has declined. His refutations of earlier Greek science are frequently based upon an insecure grasp of the texts he is refuting, and only in astrological matters does he appear to understand what he is criticising.[4] Basil makes considerable use of Aristotle, Theophrastus and Aelian.[5] Here again it is probable that intermediary

[1] G. Bardy, *Théophile d'Antioche, Trois Livres à Autolycus* (Sources chrétiennes 20, Paris 1948), p. 10. J. Geffcken (*Zwei griechischen Apologeten*, Leipzig 1907, p. 250) is very critical of Theophilus' ability; J. Tixeront (*Précis de Patrologie*, Paris 1918, p. 58f) rather less so.

[2] H.-I. Marrou, op. cit., pp. 70–80.

[3] P. Koetschau, *Origenes Werke*, i, (*G.C.S.*, Leipzig 1899) pp. xxv–xxx. For Or.'s dislike of the positivist and unspiritual nature of Aristotelian thought, see G. Bardy, *Origène et l'Aristotélisme* (Mélanges G. Glotz, i, Paris 1932, pp. 75–83).

[4] Yves Courtonne, *Saint Basile et l'Hellénisme* (Paris 1934), pp. 142–5.

[5] Mainly Aristotle, *Historia Animalium*, but also *Meteorology, de*

sources were used. K. Gronau's thesis that Basil was
acquainted with Plato's *Timaeus* only at second hand
through Posidonius[1] has not found favour in more recent
investigations.[2] It is more likely that P. J. Levie is
correct in arguing Basil's use of a zoological manual in
order to explain the admixture of fanciful matter with
genuinely Aristotelian passages in the *Hexaemeron*,[3] but
in view of Basil's education it is unlikely that he was
unfamiliar with the primary Aristotelian sources. It
remains, however, that Basil is seldom accurate or reliable and that his work, like that of Gregory of Nyssa,
is of little importance in the history of scientific thought.
Nemesius' knowledge of Galen was extensive and accurate,[4] and on occasions independent in judgment.[5] He
uses Aristotle *Historia Animalium* probably at first hand,[6]
and also the *Nicomachaean Ethics* and *De Partibus Animalium*. But this degree of serious regard for scientific
accuracy does not in itself make Nemesius a scientist.

---

caelo, de gen. et corrupt., de part. animalium and *Metaphysics*; Theophrastus, *Hist. plantarum, de causis plant., de signis tempestat.*; Aelian,
de nat. animalium.

[1] *Poseidonios und de jüdisch-christliche Genesis-exegese* (Leipzig-
Berlin 1914).

[2] e.g. Y. Courtonne, op. cit., p. 157; Stanislas Giet, *Basile de
Césarée, Homélies sur l'Hexaémeron* (Sources chrétiennes 26, Paris
1949), p. 61f.

[3] P. J. Levie, *Les Sources de la 7me et de la 8me Homélies de Saint
Basile sur l'Hexaémeron* (Musée Belge 1914(1920)), p. 133.

[4] Nemes., *de nat. hom.*, shows acquaintance with Galen, *The
Agreement between Hippocrates and Plato, On the Elements according to
Hippocrates, On the Use of Parts of the Body, On the Natural Faculties,
On the Care of the Health, On Semen, On the Purpose of Respiration.*

[5] F. S. Lammert, *Hellenistische Medizin bei Ptolemaios und Nemesios*
(Philologus xciv, 1940), pp. 125–141.

[6] So W. Telfer, *Nemesius of Emesa on the Nature of Man* (Lib.
Chr. Classics iv, London 1955), p. 305. But E. Skard, *Nemesios-
studien*, i (Symbolae Osloenses xv, Oslo 1936) regards Galen as an
intermediary source.

In company with all the Greek fathers he passed from observation of fact to the interpretation of its significance, and so passed beyond the frontiers of science into the realms of philosophy and theology.

At the centre of the interest in the natural world which
the Greek fathers exhibit stood man; partly perhaps, by
reason of his accessibility as an object of study, but
mainly because his position in the natural order was
seen to be of peculiar importance, central to the whole
of creation. There was no doubt in their minds that
man's position was firmly rooted in the natural order.
He is no phantom from another world but belongs here,
rooted in earth along with the creatures around him.
The irrational passions of greed, lust and rage exhibited
by the animal are present in man, but are transmuted
by the influence of mind, writes Gregory of Nyssa, into
the human sins of pride, covetousness and the like.[1] To
say that man is an animal whose passions are transmuted, whose body is adapted to the rational life[2] is, of
course, to say that man is not only an animal. In what
sense he is more than that is considered later.[3] At this
point we may notice some of what is said about man's
physical structure and functions, and the ailments to
which he is prone.

Important in this connection is the remarkable work
of Nemesius of Emesa entitled *On the Nature of Man*, in
which he puts forward his view of the continuity to be
discerned running through the whole of creation, the
higher orders being rooted in the lower. For Nemesius
there are no sudden leaps in nature, but a merging of
the inanimate into the plant, the plant into the irrational animal, the animal into man, man into the un-

---

[1] *de hom. opif.*, xviii. 4.   [2] ibid., viii.7f.
[3] See below, Ch. 3.

embodied spiritual beings. He takes as examples the *pinna* and what he calls the sea nettle,[1] and describes them as animals which look like plants, fixed to the bed of the sea, covered with shell as though with bark, yet possessing an animal's sense of touch. Nemesius traces the development of species through the sponge, shell fish and earthworm to creatures possessing more developed sensory perception and power of locomotion, and so to man.[2] Man's greater sensitivity of touch, especially in his finger-tips, is made possible by the delicacy of his skin and the absence of thick hair, scales or shell on his body.[3] All that the lower orders possess physically, man possesses, and man is not subject to their physical defects. Snakes and fish lack feet; crabs and lobsters lack heads, carrying their organs of perception in their breasts; some creatures lack a lung; some, such as birds, lack bladders; but man suffers from none of these deprivations.[4] Nemesius observes that this is consistent with the creation narrative in Genesis, in which man is the last creature to be made, thus summing up all that had preceded him.[5]

The patristic view of human physiology is dominated by the Stoic physiology elaborated in the second century by Galen. There is almost unquestioned agreement that the physiological function of veins is to transmit blood, which is produced by the liver, and the function of arteries to transmit *pneuma*, or spirit, which is inhaled by the lungs and warmed by the heart. On the function of the vein, Clement of Alexandria has something to say in connection with lactation: when better feeding in spring increases the blood supply of a ewe, the increase can be observed in the distension of the animal's veins.[6]

[1] The sea anemone or the coral polyp? See W. Telfer, *Lib. Christian Classics*, iv (1955), p. 233.

[2] *de nat. hom.*, i.3; based probably on a Stoic source assimilated by Galen.　　　　　　　　[3] ibid. i.6; viii.30.

[4] ibid., iv.23.　　　[5] ibid., 1.4.　　　[6] *Paed.*, i.6.50; cf. ii.10.

D

Clement makes a similar point elsewhere: food, he says, passes into the veins as blood, and the veins become greatly distended and exhibit strong pulsations.[1] The function of the artery is to transmit *pneuma*, and Clement, writing of human lactation, says that at the birth of a child blood from the veins near the mother's breast becomes mixed with '*pneuma* discharged from the neighbouring arteries' to form milk.[2] There is little attempt to define *pneuma*; it is assumed to be the vital principle of life.[3] Heat, writes Gregory of Nyssa, has its origin in the heart,[4] since loss of heat and death are seen to go together. 'From the heart, pipe-like passages which grow from one another in many ramifications diffuse through the whole body the warm and fiery *pneuma*.' Blood is produced by the liver, and is warmed 'by a muscular passage, called by those skilled in such matters the artery, which conveys the warmed air from the heart'. 'The channels of the blood, issuing from the liver as from a fountain head, accompany the warm *pneuma* everywhere throughout the body, so that one by isolation from the other may not become diseased and destroy the constitution.' The channels carrying blood from the liver start as twin passages and divide into branching channels all over the body.[5] Gregory envisages the heart as simply the source of warm air or *pneuma*. Theodoret agrees that the heart is the source of warmth, and adds that it needs cooling by the pure air inhaled through the trachea and the 'smooth passages' to the left ventricle of the heart. The air is warmed and transmitted to the lung to be expelled through the 'rough artery', presumably the trachea.[6] Theodoret

[1] *Strom.*, 1.6.44.2.

[2] ibid., i.6.39.5.

[3] See G. Verbeke, *L'Évolution de la Doctrine du Pneûma du Stoicisme à Saint Augustin* (Louvain 1945), p. 32f.

[4] *de hom. opif.*, xii.2.

[5] ibid., xxx.11f., 15, 22f.; cf. Irenaeus, *adv. haer.*, v.3.2.

[6] *de prov.*, iii, *P.G.*, 83.589cd.

differs from Gregory in associating the heart with blood as well as with air and *pneuma*. The liver draws blood from the stomach, he writes, and passes it to the heart.[1] The blood is transmitted by veins, whose walls are thin in order to permit parts adjacent to them to draw nourishment from them. Blood is thick, and the pores in the wall of a vein are large to allow its passage. Arteries, however, transmit blood and *pneuma*, and are double-walled in order to prevent the highly volatile *pneuma* from escaping prematurely. Veins are placed in close proximity to arteries, so that the warmth of the *pneuma* in the latter can ensure a proper flow of blood in the former, since blood congeals if allowed to cool.[2] Nemesius states the matter clearly in saying that the body is fed by veins, warmed by arteries, and given sensitivity by nerves[3]. Breath issuing from the mouth is 'a kind of smoke' thrown off by the heated *pneuma* in the heart.[4] On the formation of *pneuma*, Nemesius records three views: that it is vapour from the finest part of the blood drawn from the veins into the arteries; that it is air drawn from the lung to the heart; that it is air in the lung warmed by the heart.[5] In none of this is there any conception of the circulation of blood, and the beating of pulses Nemesius explains as being caused by the passage of *pneuma* through the arteries as it is pumped by the heart. He did not follow Galen in believing that arteries distribute blood as well as *pneuma*, but was aware of the presence of blood in arteries, and is prob-

[1] ibid., 593a. Cyril of Jerusalem notes that food is in part changed into blood, *Cat.*, ix.15.

[2] *de prov.*, iii, *P.G.*, 83.593d–596a. There is no evidence that Clement of Alexandria or Gregory of Nyssa were conversant at first hand with Galen's text. Theodoret, in describing arteries as conveyors of blood as well as *pneuma*, is closer to Galen's view.

[3] *de nat. hom.*, xxiv.42.

[4] ibid., xxiii.41.

[5] ibid., xxiv.42; xxviii.44.

ably relying upon the older authority of Erasistratus in saying that the heart's beat distends and contracts arteries, causing them to suck a certain amount of refined blood from neighbouring veins. Excess heat is evacuated from the arteries through the pores of the skin, and from the heart directly through the mouth and nose.[1]

Running through much of what Clement and Origen say about blood is the Levitical equation of blood with life. The equation leads Origen to the conclusion that some animals at least must be credited with souls. Those creatures, he says, which have no fluid similar to human blood possess something equivalent.[2] Clement puts it differently: blood is an original element in man, on account of which some have called it the substance of the soul. Solidified, it becomes flesh; agitated and frothed, it becomes milk. The transformation of blood into milk, he writes, can be explained in two ways: when the umbilical cord is severed at birth, the supply of blood to the foetus is checked and the blood flows instead to the breasts, changing to milk in a manner analogous to its transformation to pus in ulceration. An alternative explanation is that the muscular effort of childbirth enlarges the veins of the breast, and the resulting concentration of blood and *pneuma* in the vicinity of the breast is agitated to a frothy consistency like that of a breaking wave, though remaining essentially blood.[3] Some hold, he continues, that semen is the foam of the blood, from which he concludes that since semen goes to constitute a future human body, it is evident that blood constitutes the essence of the human body.[4]

---

[1] *de nat. hom.*, xxiv.42. Gregory of Nazianzus records that in sickness his sister's blood temperature was very high, 'agitated and boiling'. *Orat.*, viii.17.

[2] *de princ.*, ii.8.1. So Basil, *Hex.*, viii.2.168a.

[3] *Paed.*, i.6.39.4–5.   [4] ibid., i.6.48.3; 49.1.

The principle of respiration is stated by Clement of Alexandria: creatures that breathe do so by expansion of the lung towards the thorax, and thus they inhale air.[1] The lung itself is described by Cyril of Jerusalem as soft,[2] by Basil and Gregory of Nyssa as viscous and porous,[3] by Nemesius as being composed of 'frothy flesh'.[4] The lung, writes Theodoret, is like a bellows brought into operation by the contraction and expansion of the muscles at the thorax. Breath is emitted by the trachea, opening the epiglottis, and passing through the throat to the mouth. The teeth enable the sound to be formed into speech, fluency being facilitated by a gland which bubbles up like a spring, preventing the tongue from drying. Theodoret describes the lung as being like a soft blanket, spongy, porous and filled with passages.[5] Nemesius gives a rather more detailed account of the vocal organs themselves, 'composed of three large structures of gristle', leading to the pharynx and the mouth.[6] Basil explains the function of the lungs, to ventilate and to cool interior heat.[7] Gregory of Nyssa expands this: the heart, whose function is to supply warmed *pneuma* to the body, receives its air from the lungs which in turn are supplied through the windpipe. The heart is situated at the back of the lungs, and by expansion and contraction draws to itself a supply of air much as bellows draw air to a furnace. The action is spontaneous.[8] The lungs also force air up the windpipe, and as the air strikes against the membranous protuberances which divide this flute-like passage 'in a circular arrangement', it utters a sound in the manner of a flute. The resonance is increased by the palate,

[1] *Strom.*, vii.6.32.2.
[2] *Cat.*, xii.30.
[3] *Hex.*, vii.1.149b; *de hom. opif.*, xxx.16.
[4] *de nat. hom.*, xxviii.44.
[5] *de prov.*, iii, *P.G.*, 83.589b; 593a.
[6] *de nat. hom.*, xxviii.44.   [7] *Hex.*, vii.1.149b.
[8] *de hom opif.*, xxx.15f; xxx.2; Nemesius, *de nat. hom.*, xxviii.44.

which receives the sound on to its concave surface and divides it by the two passages that extend to the nostrils, and by the cartilages about the perforated bone.[1] Gregory says also that grief causes a constriction and contraction of many organs, which presses on the lungs and gives rise to violent drawing of breath in the endeavour to widen what has contracted.[2]

Clement of Alexandria cites the authority of 'physicians' for the opinion that the brain is naturally cold, and that anointing the breast and nostrils allows the vapour to warm the chill of the brain. This practice evaporates the effusions of the brain and induces sleep.[3] Gregory of Nyssa describes the brain receiving sensory impressions, sorting out the impressions like people in a city going their ways to various streets.[4] A question which taxes Gregory is whether mind is seated in the brain or the heart. At first he inclines to favour the heart, though he admits the alternative to be supported 'by plausible superficialities'. The brain, he writes, sends sensitive nerve-processes down the vertebrae of the neck to the isthmoidal passage, and unites them with the muscles there. 'I do not reject the statement, similar to that which I hear from those who spend their time on anatomical research, that the cerebral membrane, enfolding itself in the brain and steeped in the vapours that arise from it, forms a foundation for the senses'.[5] Mental aberrations do not arise, as Gregory says we are well aware, from mere heaviness of head, but skilled physicians declare that man's mind is also weakened by disease in the membranes of the brain. The name of the disease is called frenzy, derived from the name of the membranes, φρένες.[6] Within a few pages Gregory

---

[1] *de hom. opif.*, ix.3.

[2] ibid., xii.4; cf. Nemesius, *de nat. hom.*, xxviii.44.

[3] *Paed.*, ii.8.   [4] *de hom. opif.*, x.3f.

[5] So also Theodoret, *Graec. affect. cur.*, v.81.

[6] *de hom. opif.*, xii.1–5.

seems to have argued himself into upholding the supremacy of the brain. The supreme force in the body's economy, he says, is the cerebral membrane. The brain is nourished by the purest heat and fluid. The moistened membrane stretches downwards like a pipe, extending through the successive vertebrae, and is coterminous with the base of the spine, giving power and motion to the whole body, being protected by bone.[1] In much of this Gregory is paralleled by Theodoret, who adds that the brain is protected by the cranium. But lest the soft fluid brain should be damaged by impact with the bone of the cranium, it is protected by two coverings of membrane, of which the inner is the more delicate in structure.[2] Nemesius places the seat of imagination in the frontal lobes of the brain and the nerves proceeding from them. The senses feed data to the appropriate part of the brain, in which takes place the act of sensory perception.[3] In the case of smell the brain is not connected to the nose by a sensory nerve, but receives the sense data direct from the nostrils on to its front surface.[4] The organ of intellect is the middle of the brain.[5] Memory functions in the cerebellum or posterior lobe of the brain. Observation shows, writes Nemesius, that if the front of the brain suffers any kind of lesion the senses are impaired; injury to the cerebellum affects memory; injury to the middle brain impairs intellect. Injury to all three parts may result in death.[6] Following Galen, Nemesius says that the hard motor nerves pro-

[1] ibid., xxx.24.

[2] de prov., iii, P.G., 83.601ab.

[3] de nat. hom., vi.27. Nemesius expands this statement, viii.30 on touch; ix.31 on taste.

[4] ibid., xi. The passages from the nostrils to the brain can become blocked if the subject suffers from a head cold, resulting in loss of the sense of smell (ibid., vi. 27), but the brain is protected by a perforated bone like a sieve or sponge (ibid., xxviii.44).

[5] ibid., xii.32.

[6] ibid., xiii, based largely on Galen.

ceed from the posterior lobe to the marrow of the spine.
The further down the spine from the brain, the harder
are the nerves that spring from it, branching out in pairs
from each vertebra.[1] Following Galen and Aristotle, he
notes that all sensory organs are double. That even
tongues are double is plain, he writes, from observation
of the tongue of a snake, which is not a single tongue
split but basically a double organ, deriving its sensitivity
from the front of the brain. Sensation is vital to survival,
in Nemesius' view, and is therefore dispersed by the
nervous system throughout the body, only bone, horn,
hair, nail and gristle being insensitive. The nervous
system is almost an extension of brain through the
body.[2] The Cappadocian fathers have no doubt of the
importance of the senses, apart from their function of
enabling man to enjoy the pleasures of life.[3] The senses
link body and soul,[4] an idea which may be associated
with that elaborated by Basil, who follows Aristotle in
seeing sensation as the first stage of knowledge. Sensation leads to the successive formation of image, concept
and word.[5] Basil puts this to the test in his discussion of
Platonic astronomical observations. Having outlined
Plato's views as expressed in the *Timaeus*, Basil checks
their truth by asking the important question: what evidence do the senses give to support such ideas?[6] Athenagoras and Gregory of Nyssa consider the working of
the senses during sleep. The senses are only relaxed,
writes Athenagoras, and suffer an interruption of their
normal functioning.[7] Gregory says that the warm vapours
which fill the body during sleep penetrate the organs of
sense and render them inactive, though mental processes continue. Digestion, continuing through sleep,

---

[1] *de nat. hom.*, xxvii.43.   [2] ibid., viii.30.

[3] Greg. Nyssa, *de hom. opif.*, xxx.2.

[4] ibid., xiv.2.   [5] *Hex.*, iii.1.56a.

[6] *Hex.*, iii.3.57c.

[7] *de res. mort.*, xvi.

keeps the senses partially active, in a condition similar to that of a lyre with slackened strings.[1]

The ear, writes Clement of Alexandria, performs the purely physical function of expelling dirt.[2] But although the ear functions through the physical passages of the head, hearing involves more than simply physical functioning. Psychical perception and intelligence distinguish significant sound from non-significant.[3] Gregory of Nyssa and Theodoret also write of the part played by the mind in hearing, noting in particular the wonder of selective hearing.[4] Gregory of Nazianzus says that excessive noise impairs hearing.[5] The organ of hearing, writes Nemesius, is the soft aural nerve from the brain, and the gristle in the ears, the latter being especially suitable for picking up sounds.[6]

Vision, says Basil, travels from the eye to the object seen, intervening light allowing vision to reach its object. Distance affects the size of objects seen, the sun, for example, appearing only a cubit in diameter, because human vision cannot traverse the great intervening space and becomes used up, only reaching its object in an enfeebled condition. From this Basil concludes that human vision is unreliable.[7] Arguing from the way in which a half-submerged oar appears to be broken, Nemesius too regards vision as unreliable when unsupported by other senses and mental faculties.[8] Gregory of Nyssa expresses a similar idea to that of Basil in saying that the eye sees light by having light within itself to

---

[1] de hom. opif., xiii.3, 7f.

[2] Paed., ii.10; so Nemesius, de nat. hom., xxiii.41.

[3] Strom., vii.7.31.5.

[4] Greg. Nyssa, de hom. opif., x.3; Theodoret, de prov., iii, P.G., 83.605a.

[5] Orat., xxvii.4.

[6] de nat. hom., x.

[7] Hex., ii.7.45a; vi.9.140a.

[8] de nat. hom., vii.29; cf. Origen's opinion that distorted vision gives rise to distorted judgment, Comm. in Cant., i.4.

take hold of the kindred light outside.[1] Nemesius, after giving a summary of several classical theories of vision, follows Aristotle in saying that vision touches the object observed at only one point at a time, and that what it observes is primarily colour. In practice it relies on the co-operation of other mental faculties, such as memory, and of the other senses.[2] Brilliant light affects vision. Basil observes that after gazing at glaring objects, eyes find relief in returning to blues and greens.[3] After darkness, writes Novatian, the brilliance of sudden sunshine does not really give light but rather increases the blindness; gradual sunrise thus enables our eyes to grow accustomed to sunlight.[4] Origen says that the eye is dilated when looking at large objects, contracted when looking at small ones.[5] The function of the eyelash, writes Gregory of Nyssa, is to shade the eye from strong light,[6] the faculty of vision remaining active even when the eye is covered by a closed lid.[7] Theodoret includes among the protective devices round the eyes not merely the eyebrows and lashes, but also 'the moist coating fed from the brain to the eyes through the glands at their corners'.[8]

Of the nose, Theodoret says that it has a twofold function: first, a selective function of accepting agreeable smells and rejecting disagreeable; secondly, that of releasing through the nostrils vapours which are harmful to the brain.[9] Clement of Alexandria sees its func-

---

[1] *de infant.* These views probably have their origin in the Stoic doctrine that sight is a material emanation from the eye; cf. Plotinus, *Enn.*, ii.8.1, and Plato's account in the *Timaeus* of two currents of light meeting, one from the eye, the other from the object.

[2] *de nat. hom.*, vii.29.   [3] *Ep.*, 24.

[4] *de Trin.*, xviii; so also Cyril of Jerus., *Cat.*, ix.8.

[5] *de princ.*, i.1.6.   [6] *de infant.*

[7] *de virg.*, xii.

[8] *de prov.*, iii, *P.G.*, 83.601d–604c.

[9] ibid., 604d–605a.

tion to be the expelling of mucus,[1] and in reverse, the admitting of suitable vapours to the brain, on account of which he recommends anointing of the nostrils to warm the inhaled air.[2] He also regards air inhaled through the nostrils as being purer than air inhaled through the mouth.[3]

The organ of taste, writes Nemesius, is the tip of the tongue, reinforced by the palate, from which spread nerves to the brain,[4] an opinion contradicted by Gregory of Nyssa, who holds the function of the tongue to be primarily to facilitate speech and also to guide food between the teeth.[5] Taste, he says, is largely a matter of memory; the distinction between bitter and sweet is made by the faculty of memory.[6] Here Gregory may be following Origen's view of the importance of experience. If artificially-made honey were produced, he says, no-one could tell that it had not been made by bees.[7]

The process of digestion is described in almost identical terms by Athenagoras and Theodoret. They describe it as a twofold process, taking place first in the stomach, from which part of the food is evacuated. When the food retained by the stomach is digested, it passes to the liver, where there takes place a further separation of useful from useless, with disposal of the latter. The food retained by the liver is then dispersed to various parts of the body, where it is assimilated;[8] distributed, adds Chrysostom, between warmth, blood, fluid and bile, but he admits that he does not know how.[9]

---

[1] *Paed.*, ii.10. [2] ibid., ii.8.

[3] *Strom.*, vii.6.31.9. [4] *de nat. hom.*, ix.31.

[5] *Antirrhet. c. Eunom.* (= *c. Eunom.*, xiib); *de hom. opif.*, viii.8.

[6] ibid., x.6.

[7] *c. Cels.*, iv.73.

[8] Athenag., *de res. mort.*, v; Theodoret, *de prov.*, iii, *P.G.*, 83.593b; cf. Origen, *de princ.*, ii.1.4; Cyril of Jerus., *Cat.*, ix.15. Note the reference by Greg. Nyssa to 'circulation of food' (*de infant*), and to the retention and evacuation of food (*de hom. opif.*, xxx.18).

[9] *de incomp.*, 1, *P.G.*, 48.704c.

Nemesius adds two points to this account, noting first
the muscular action of the gullet in stretching up and
sucking down the food, and secondly, that the liver is
the organ most suited to the function of transforming
food into blood because its own substance is blood-like.[1]
Bad digestion, in the opinion of Clement of Alexandria,
is caused by soft beds.[2] Theodoret makes the anatomical
point that the stomach lies in front of the spine in order
to allow distension forwards when food has been taken.[3]

Solid matter rejected by the liver passes to the bowels,
which, says Gregory of Nyssa, revolve the matter in
their manifold windings and for a time retain it. This
slow process of evacuation prevents rapid recurrence of
appetite and perpetual feeding such as one observes in
animals.[4] Digestion is 'a kind of melting of materials as
in a foundry', the source of heat being the heart. For
Clement of Alexandria too, heat caused by bodily
movement brings about digestion. Where movement is
insufficient, heat is lacking, and the food remains like a
loaf in a cold oven. Accordingly, the faeces are in excess
in the case of those who do not eliminate excrement by
rubbing down after exercise.[5] Nemesius, in accordance
with Galen's view of bodily health as consisting of a
balance of qualities, explains evacuation of the bowels
as an involuntary restoring of balance by eliminating
excess,[6] and includes in this balancing process every
organ which eliminates excess matter, bladder, pores,
eyes, ears and mouth. Some of these organs can be said
to function in a fully involuntary manner, but this is
only partly true of the bowels, over which man has
some muscular control.[7] Basil suffered from bowel com-

---

[1] *de nat. hom.*, xxiii.41.   [2] *Paed.*, ii.9.

[3] *de prov.*, iii, *P.G.*, 83.600b.

[4] *de hom. opif.*, xxx.21.

[5] *Paed.*, iii.11.   [6] *de nat. hom.*, i.6.

[7] ibid., xxvii.43. It is perhaps only fair to relegate to the obscurity
of a footnote Novatian's description of a man playing the pipes

plaints, and writes to a fellow bishop that he is kept indoors by diarrhoea and rebellions of the bowels, which drench him like recurring waves.[1] The following year he writes to the physician Meletius that he intends to stay indoors until the spring in order not to cause a recurrence of his complaint.[2] Chrysostom points out the inadvisability of giving bitter purgatives to patients suffering from weak bowels, in case the medicine should aggravate the weakness.[3]

Diet should be balanced. For Nemesius this follows from Galen's insistence on proper balance; in cases of sickness the physician diagnoses the respect in which the body is suffering excess and restores the balance by prescribing a corrective diet.[4] Thus, writes Nemesius, when concupiscence reaches a point of unbalance it can be cured by a physician, 'who must win it over, as far as possible, to its normal temperament, by suitable diet', as well as by prescribing exercise and even drugs.[5] Novatian says that meat was added to man's original diet of fruit as cultivation of the soil demanded more robust food.[6] Food in the wrong quantity and of conflicting kinds, writes Origen, breeds fevers in the body, and he adds that moderate and balanced eating is hardly to be expected from human beings.[7] Gregory of Nyssa and Nemesius note that the diet of pregnant women affects the growth of the foetus,[8] and Origen

and drawing breath with some effort from the bowels (*de spect.*, v)· His knowledge of anatomy was not strong.

[1] *Ep.*, 162.   [2] *Ep.*, 193.

[3] *Comm. in Rom.*, ix (Rom. v.11).

[4] *de nat. hom.*, i.6.

[5] ibid., xvii.36; cf. Origen on a correct diet in the treatment of defective vision. He adds that the benefit may not be felt at once, *Hom. in Jesu Nave*, xx.2.

[6] *de cib. jud.*, ii.

[7] *de princ.*, ii.10.4; iii.2.2.; cf. Greg. Nyssa, *de virg.*, xxii.

[8] Greg. Nyssa, *c. Eunom.*, i.39; Nemesius, *de nat. hom.*, xl.57; Origen, *c. Cels.*, iv.18.

that in youth food contributes to growth, but when growth is complete food preserves life.[1] Clement of Alexandria warns against over-feeding children: their bodies are made to grow straight by deficiency of food, for thus the *pneuma* which pervades the body and causes growth is not checked by excess food.[2]

Amid frequent patristic denunciations of the evils of strong drink, it is interesting to find Clement writing that wine is permissible for physic, for health, for relaxation and for enjoyment. Wine makes the drinker more benignant than before, more agreeable to his friends and kinder to his servants. But excessive drink affects speech, vision and balance.[3] Novatian notes the effect of alcohol on an empty stomach,[4] Clement its effect on the liver,[5] and Chrysostom its effect on a man's vision the day following his excess.[6]

We find constant appeals for plainness of diet. Clement of Alexandria recommends bulbs, olives, herbs, milk, cheese, fruit, honey-combs, no sauces or cooked food and roast meat in preference to boiled. Plainness of food, he says, is conducive to good digestion and lightness of body, whereas stomach disorders are caused 'by the unhappy arts of cookery and pastry making'. He objects to the emasculation of bread by straining off the nourishing part of the grain.[7] Basil too will have no cooking in his house,[8] though he can hardly have adhered rigidly to this rule: he is delighted when Phalerius sends him some fresh-water fish, having nursed a grudge against them ever since they escaped

[1] *de princ.*, ii.11.7; cf. Methodius, *de res.*, on the threefold function of food, to warm, to build blood and to build flesh.

[2] *Paed.*, ii.1; cf. Tertullian, *de ieiun.*, xvii.

[3] *Paed.*, ii.2.

[4] *de cib. jud.*, iii.

[5] *Paed.*, ii.2.

[6] *Comm. in Rom.*, xiii (Rom. viii.5–7).

[7] *Paed.*, ii.1.

[8] *Ep.*, 41.

him beneath the ice.[1] Gregory of Nazianzus describes
Basil's diet as consisting of bread, salt and water,[2] with
which we may compare Basil's own references to his
diet. In one letter he writes of bread, water and vegetables;[3] in another he implies that fruit and fish are also
eaten;[4] in another he adds sour wine;[5] and to Amphilochius he stipulates that any vegetables that are bought
must be cheap.[6] This plainness of diet, he claims, prevents the dulling of the faculties, but we may note his
frequent stomach disorders. It is entertaining to find
Gregory of Nazianzus begging vegetables from Amphilochius, 'plenty of them, and the best, for I am going to
receive the great Basil, and you who have had experience of him full-fed and philosophical would not like to
know him hungry and irritated'.[7] Gregory's next letter
shows that the result of his appeal for supplies was
disappointing.

Before passing to the reproductive functions of the
body, it is worth noting that Gregory of Nyssa and
Nemesius agree that the sensation resulting from grief is
experienced not in the heart, as was commonly said, but
in the stomach. Nemesius places the sensation just
below 'the cartilage in the middle of the chest, known
as the sword-shaped cartilage'. Since it has its seat in the
pit of the stomach, fear can cause vomiting.[8] Gregory
accounts for the sallow complexion of those who suffer
grief by saying that grief causes a general bodily contraction which makes bile pour on to the entrance of the
stomach.[9] For Nemesius bile is generated by the gall
bladder and the spleen,[10] the latter pouring excess black

---

[1] *Ep.*, 329.
[2] *Orat.*, xlii.61.
[3] *Ep.*, 2.
[4] *Ep.*, 14.
[5] *Ep.*, 41.
[6] *Ep.*, 236.
[7] *Ep.*, 25.
[8] *de nat. hom.*, xx.40.
[9] *de hom. opif.*, xii.2, 4. The condition of the bile affects dreams, ibid., xiii.16.
[10] *de nat. hom.*, xxiii.41.

bile into the stomach.[1] Exhalations rising from the disturbed bile to the heart have the effect of overheating the heart, causing anger.[2]

The urge to sexual intercourse, writes Origen, arises from the need of the male body to empty certain passages which are filled with semen, the emission of fluid sometimes taking place spontaneously.[3] Nemesius attributes the stimulation to a pungent fluid which flows from the kidneys;[4] Clement of Alexandria attributes it to the body's failure to sweat and consequent retention of superfluous fluid which in part flows to the testicles, exciting lust.[5] Conception takes place, he says, when the semen is mixed with the pure residue left by the menstrual flow, the semen coagulating the substance of the blood, much as rennet curdles milk. A proper proportion of male to female fluid is essential if conception is to take place; excess of either leads to sterility. Some hold, Clement continues, that semen is the foam of the blood, which is agitated by the natural heat of the male and deposited in the seminal passages.[6] The womb is situated beneath the bladder but above the intestine called the rectum, and extends its neck between the shoulders of the bladder. The mouth of this neck, into which the semen passes, is closed when filled and thus rendered useless, only to be opened by the process of birth. Thus the womb, by its natural closing, rejects coition during pregnancy.[7] In Nemesius' view blood is transformed into semen in veins and arteries primarily for their own sustenance and secondarily for the purpose of intercourse. Semen, he says, is carried first to the

---

[1] *de nat. hom.*, xxviii.45.

[2] ibid., xxi.40; cf. Galen's pathology based on the theory of humours: blood, phlegm, black and yellow bile. Greg. Nyssa associates black bile with anger (*c. Eunom.*, i.1); Basil associates it with nausea at sea (*Ep.*, 2).

[3] *de princ.*, iii.4.3; so Nemesius, *de nat. hom.*, xxv.42.

[4] ibid., xxviii.45.   [5] *Paed.*, iii.11.

[6] ibid., i.6.48.1–3.   [7] ibid., ii.10.

head, from which it follows that the severing of 'veins that run round the ears and alongside the carotid arteries' produces sterility. The semen passes down to 'a spiral and varicose system enveloping the scrotum', and into the testicles. *Pneuma* is added to the semen from an artery. Evidence that semen is carried by a vein is to be observed in emission of blood as a result of excessive copulation.[1]

Of contraception Origen writes that those who desire coition without conception cast contempt upon the nature of human generation.[2] Athenagoras and Chrysostom regard abortion as murder.[3] Basil rejects any fine distinction between a formed and an unformed foetus as being 'inadmissible among us'. Abortion ranks also as suicide, since, he says, such attempts are usually fatal to the mother as well,[4] and women who administer drugs to procure abortions are murderesses.

Mention has already been made of Clement's account of lactation, by which blood is transformed into milk.[5] He says also that the blood loses its colour and becomes white in order not to frighten the child.[6] Food eaten by a nursing mother, says Origen, changes into milk to suit the child's needs.[7]

Bone is described by Gregory of Nyssa as filled with marrow, its joints held by sinews and ligaments; it receives nourishment but is insensitive.[8] Theodoret says that the unique upright posture of man derives from his bone structure. The spine, he writes, consists of a strong column of vertebrae extending as far as the neck,

---

[1] *de nat. hom.*, xxv.42, following Galen.

[2] *c. Cels.*, v.42.

[3] Athenag., *supplic.*, xxxv; Chrysost., *Comm. in Rom.* xxiv (Rom. xiii.14).

[4] *Ep.*, 188.   [5] See above, p. 44.

[6] *Strom.*, i.6.39.2.

[7] *c. Cels.*, iv.18; cf. Greg. Nyssa, *c. Eunom.*, i.27.

[8] *de hom. opif.*, xxx.7; *antirrhet. c. Eunom.* (= *c. Eunom.*, xii.6); cf. Tatian, *Orat. ad Graec.*, xii.

E

holding in place shoulders, neck, arms and head. The
spine is articulated so that it does not break when a man
bends. The marrow of the spine has its origin in the
brain.[1] Theodoret describes the structure of the leg
briefly—constructed of three sections, jointed at hip,
knee and ankle, each joint being bound with tendons
and muscles[2]—and the hand in greater detail. The
wrist, he says, links the forearm with the metacarpal
bones, which terminate in five fingers. The fingers are
each divided into three sections separated by joints. Of
the extremities of these bones he says that some are
concave, some convex; the convex end of one bone fits
into the concavity of that next to it, the two being held
together by tendons. Each joint is enclosed in muscle
to facilitate movement, and the skin surrounding the
fingers is thin in order not to impede their movement.
The nails are to protect the soft ends of the fingers, and
are therefore different in function from the claws of an
animal, which are instruments of aggression. Later,
Theodoret notes the use of the hand for gripping, made
possible by the opposition of finger and thumb.[3]

According to Nemesius, hair is composed of vapours
which have congealed as they issued from the pores of
the skin.[4] Clement of Alexandria says that women who
dye their grey hair increase its greyness since the cos-
metics they use dry the hair. Greyness indicates a defect
of heat. A change of colour does not mean that the
substance of the hair has changed, only its colour.[5]

Two references to teeth may be worth noting: Basil
writes to thank Amphilochius for a gift of sweetmeats:
'It is not for me at my age to be munching, since my
teeth have long ago been worn away by time and ill-
health.'[6] Basil was at the time forty-six years of age.

---

[1] de prov., iii, P.G., 83.600b.   [2] ibid., 597bc.
[3] ibid., iv, P.G., 83.613a–c; 621c.
[4] de nat. hom., xxviii.45.
[5] Paed., i.6.44.3; ii.8.   [6] Ep., 233.

Gregory of Nazianzus had still got his teeth at the age of thirty-two, and refers to the difficulty they experience in biting Basil's hunks of bread.[1]

Theodoret was concerned during his episcopacy of Cyrrhus for the bodily as well as the spiritual welfare of his flock. In a spirited *apologia* for his actions as bishop, he describes how, in his concern for public health, he made himself responsible for the public baths, and when he found that the river was insufficient to provide drainage for the town, he built a drain to augment the water flow.[2] He also wrote letters recommending the presbyter Peter, who had practised medicine for a long time in Cyrrhus and in Alexandria, and was a man of excellent character. Theodoret says that his own practice had been to encourage those skilled in medicine. 'I beg your magnificence to look after this man. He is well fitted to help the sick.'[3]

Gregory of Nazianzus describes Basil in his student days at Athens, turning to the study of medicine after mastering astronomy, geometry and mathematics. He embarked upon his medical studies partly, Gregory tells us, by reason of his own physical delicacy, and partly because of his concern for the sick, and he attained proficiency not only in its practice, but also in its theory and principles.[4] Gregory's brother Caesarius also studied medicine 'in so far as it treats of physiology, correct balance within the human body, and the causes of disease, in order to remove their roots and so destroy their offspring with them'.[5] Harnack gives a list of others associated with the practice of medicine, all of whom were Christians, orthodox or heretical.[6]

---

[1] *Ep.*, 5.   [2] *Ep.*, 81, *P.G.*, 83.1261c.
[3] *Ep.*, 114, 115, *P.G.*, 83.1324ab.
[4] *Orat.*, xlii.23.   [5] ibid., vii.7.
[6] A. Harnack, *Medicinisches aus der ältesten Kirchengeschichte*, T.U., viii.4, pp. 40–7 (Leipzig 1892). Alexander, a Phrygian martyr; Galen's disciples in Rome about A.D. 200, noted for their study

Basil describes medicine as a science,[1] as does Eusebius: 'We see men scientifically healing sufferers, the physicians having by much patience and training acquired the doctrines of the healing art, and conducting all their operations according to reason.'[2] Gregory of Nyssa is aware of the danger of hasty diagnosis: 'In bodily diseases, when some corrupt humour spreads unseen beneath the pores, before the unhealthy secretion has been defeated on the skin, physicians do not use such treatment as would harden the flesh, but wait till all that lurks within comes out upon the surface, and then, with the disease unmasked, apply their remedies.'[3] Chrysostom distinguishes between the various kinds of treatment given to a patient at different stages of a single complaint.[4]

Disagreements within the medical profession should not discourage a patient. The science of medicine is useful, Origen writes, although there are many differences of opinion about how to treat bodies, and there are medical opinions branded as heretical by Greeks and Barbarians alike; yet no-one would avoid medicine because of such disagreements.[5] The patient must have confidence in the physician, and Theophilus asks whether a cure is possible in the absence of confidence.[6]

---

of Aristotle and Theophrastus; Proculus; Julius Africanus, whose *Kestoi* contains medical material; Zenobius of Sidon, 'that best of physicians'; Theodotus of Laodicea, who according to Eusebius 'had reached the first rank in the healing of bodies'; a nameless Christian bishop near the sea of Tiberias, who was a physician; Flavius, tutor in Diocletian's palace at Nicomedia, and author of *de medicinalibus*; Hierakas, an Egyptian ascetic; Eusebius of Rome, a physician and son of a physician; Basil of Ancyra; Aetius the Arian.

[1] *Ep.*, 189.
[2] *Prae. Evang.*, i.5.15a; cf. Greg. Nyssa, *de virg.*, xxiii; *de hom. opif.*, xxx.1.
[3] *cat. magn.*, xxix.
[4] *Comm. in Rom.*, prol.
[5] *c. Cels.*, iii.12.
[6] *ad Autol.*, i.8.

The patient may not understand the scientific theory of medicine, says Eusebius, but his cure depends not upon his understanding but upon hope and faith.[1] Falsehoods may be acceptable on the lips of a physician.[2] Basil, perhaps from personal experience, can describe the disagreeable aspect of a physician's work, 'bending over the sick and breathing in the foul smells in order that he may heal the sick',[3] yet, adds Gregory of Nyssa, not catching the disease but healing it.[4] Elsewhere Gregory refers to those who contract ophthalmia by frequent contact with others already suffering from it.[5] Chrysostom too is less confident of the immunity of the physician and notes that the careful physician washes himself as well as his patient.[6] He also describes the physician continuing his work despite the violent opposition of a patient who kicks and spits when his tumour is bathed.[7] Gregory of Nyssa writes of the behaviour of different patients suffering from an eye complaint, 'one undergoing all that medicine can do for him, however painful; the other indulging without restraint in bathing and drinking wine'.[8] Gregory of Nazianzus contrasts two physicians: one, his brother Caesarius, 'who placed the humane practice of his art at the disposal of the authorities free of cost. All entrusted their precious charges to his care without requiring him to take the Hippocratic oath'.[9] Of the other, Gregory says that it would be well for the man's patient to accept Christian baptism while there is still

---

[1] *Prae. Evang.*, i.5.15a.

[2] Origen., *c. Cels.*, iv.19.   [3] *Ep.*, 8.

[4] *Ep.*, xvii.   [5] *c. Eunom.*, i.4.

[6] *de incomp.*, ii, *P.G.*, 48.718c; *Comm. in Rom.*, vii (Rom. iii.31).

[7] *de incomp.*, ii, *P.G.*, 48.718b.

[8] *de infant.* The sick ask for wine, writes Cyril of Jerusalem, and if it be given at the wrong time it causes delirium and two evils follow: the patient dies and the physician gets the blame. (*procat.*, xii).

[9] *Orat.*, vii.10.

time, 'before the physician is powerless to help you and
is giving you only hours to live—hours which are not his
to give—and is holding your salvation in the balance
with a nod of his head, discoursing learnedly about your
complaint after you are gone, putting up his fee by
calling in second opinions, or hinting at despair'.[1]

Among references to specific ailments we find Gregory
of Nyssa referring to the helplessness of a physician
before a cancerous condition 'because the disease is too
strong for him to deal with', and comparing the views
of an opponent to 'a swelling of humours secreted by
some dropsical inflation'.[2] Basil describes Gregory of
Nazianzus suffering from a chill in addition to his
kidney complaint.[3] Origen claims that Job suffered from
elephantiasis, though elsewhere he refers to Job's boils
in more orthodox fashion.[4] Clement of Alexandria
writes of enervation caused by over-coition as an incur-
able disease, and follows Abderis in calling it 'little
epilepsy'.[5] Gregory of Nyssa describes a fevered condition: the heart's motion heats the body and works the
lungs, therefore temperature rises and breathing becomes more rapid.[6] Gregory of Nazianzus recalls his
father's whole frame on fire with burning fever,[7] and
Basil writes of his own fevered condition by comparing
his body to a burnt wick.[8] Theodoret notes that the
pulse of a patient indicates the course of a fever, and
that temperature can be lowered by inducing vomiting,
by drugs and by blood-letting.[9] Cold drinks should not
be given to fevered patients, writes Chrysostom, despite
their demands. All the physician can do, however, is to
prohibit; he cannot enforce his advice if the patient will

---

[1] *Orat.*, xl.11.   [2] *c. Eunom.*, vii.2; ii.7.
[3] *Ep.*, 225.
[4] ἀγρίῳ ἐλέφαντι, *c. Cels.*, vi.43; *Hom. in Exod.*, vii.2.
[5] *Paed.*, ii.10.   [6] *de hom. opif.*, xxx.17.
[7] *Orat.*, xviii.28.   [8] *Ep.*, 138.
[9] *de prov.*, iv., *P.G.*, 83.620c.

not obey him.[1] He also observes that inflamed wounds
and ulcers are too painful to be touched with the hand
and have to be bathed with a fine sponge.[2] Gregory of
Nazianzus, describing his father's sickness, says that his
palate and the whole upper surface of his mouth was so
painfully ulcerated that it was with difficulty that he
could swallow even water. The skill of the physicians
was of no avail.[3]

Of anaesthetics Basil says that it would be a good
thing if ecclesiastics were to adopt the advice of the
physicians. When their patients suffer excessive pain,
they contrive for them an anaesthetic (ἀναισθησία) to
make them insensitive to their sufferings. So shall we
pray for some analgesia (ἀναλγησία) to render our souls
insensible to their ills.[4] Basil presumably refers to the
opiates listed in his *Hexaemeron*: mandrake to induce
sleep; opium to 'soften the violence of bodily ailments';
hemlock to reduce the sexual urge; hellebore to 'master
many chronic diseases'. Hemlock, hellebore, monks-
hood, mandrake and poppy juice he also refers to as
poisons.[5] Clement of Alexandria covers slightly different
ground: ivy he describes as cooling; nux as emitting a
stupefying vapour; narcissus induces torpor. The efflu-
vium of violets and roses is used to relieve and prevent
headaches; crocus and cypress are conducive to sleep.[6]
Tatian admits the beneficial properties of drugs somewhat reluctantly: there are diseases and disturbances of
the matter that is in us which can indeed be healed by
medicine; but even if you are cured by drugs (I grant
you the point from courtesy) you should attribute the
cure to God.[7] Gregory of Nyssa says that in the case of

---

[1] *Comm. in Rom.*, xii (Rom. vii.9).

[2] *de incomp.*, ii, *P.G.*, 48.718ab.

[3] *Orat.*, xviii.28.   [4] *Ep.*, 34.

[5] *Hex.*, v.4.101b-d.   [6] *Paed.*, ii.8.

[7] *Orat. ad. Graec.*, xvi; xviii; xx; cf. Clem. of Alex., *Strom.*,
vi.17.148.

those who are selling harmful drugs, a very slight experiment guarantees to the buyer the destructive power latent in the drug.[1]

Clement of Alexandria lists a few types of ointment: susinian ointment, compounded of various kinds of lily, is 'warming, aperient, drawing, moistening, abstergent, subtle, antibilious, emollient'; ointment made from narcissus is, he says, equally beneficial, but he does not specify its virtues; myrtle ointment is a styptic, stopping effusions from the body. Ointment of roses is cooling.[2] Sterner measures might be necessary: suppose that in the case of a tumour, writes Origen, we have administered dressings of oil and have treated the ailment with plasters and soothing dressings, and that the tumour resists treatment, we can only have recourse to surgery.[3] Clement writes of a good physician treating some of his patients with plasters; some with massage; some with bathing; in one case making an incision with a lancet, in another case cauterizing, in another amputating.[4] The Cappadocian fathers recognise cautery as a disagreeable necessity. Gregory of Nazianzus warns the physician against letting the patient's wishes influence his decisions, for he may have to use cautery or the knife.[5] Gregory of Nyssa and Chrysostom describe the patient shrinking from the pain of cautery and surgery, and Gregory writes of the cauterizing of warts as not being painless, though causing pain is not the purpose of the operation.[6] Origen regards the element of pain differently: cautery, he says, can be used as a threat to make the patient observe his diet and obey instructions.[7]

[1] *antirrhet. c. Eunom.* (= *c. Eunom.*, xiib).
[2] *Paed.*, ii.8.
[3] *Hom. in Jesu Nave.*, vii.6; cf. *c. Cels.*, iii.60.
[4] *Protrept.*, i.8.2.
[5] *Orat.*, ii.18.
[6] Greg. Nyssa, *Cat. magn.*, xxvi; Chrysost., *Comm. in Rom.*, ix (Rom, v.11).   [7] *c. Cels.*, vi.56; iv.72.

Mentioning cautery and amputation in another passage, he adds that bodily suffering is of spiritual value,[1] his belief in daemonic possession as a cause of sickness possibly leading him to think of the pain of cautery or surgery as being suffered by the daemon and therefore expelling it.[2]

The man who looks after his body, writes Theodoret, has the less need of physicians,[3] and Chrysostom similarly points out that a body which is out of condition is more open to disease than when properly cared for.[4] Recommending that exercise should be taken in order to produce a healthy body and a courageous soul, Clement of Alexandria advises it before meals, not after.[5]

[1] *de princ.*, ii.10.6.

[2] ibid., iii.2.2; *c. Cels.*, vii.67; viii.58f.

[3] *de prov.*, iii, *P.G.*, 83.588b.

[4] *Comm. in Rom.*, xx (Rom. xii.3); cf. xxiv (Rom. xiii.14).

[5] *Paed.*, iii.10. Ps.-Justin, *ep. ad. Zenam et Seren.*, xi, also recommends walking. Clem. Alex., refers to playing ball, for which game there were recognised rules (*Strom.*, ii.6.25.4), and Greg. Nyssa describes in some detail the game often known as pig-in-the-middle (*Ep.*, xii). Other forms of exercise referred to by the fathers include fencing (Clem. Alex., *Strom.*, ii.6.25.4); wrestling (Orig., *Comm. in Cant.*, Prol. ii; Greg. Nyssa, *c. Eunom.*, ii.15; Greg. Naz., *Orat.*, ii.85); boxing (Basil, *Ep.*, 210); swimming in the sea (Basil, *Ep.*, 293); track running (Orig., *Comm. in Cant.*, Prol. ii; cf. Basil, *ad nean.*); horse racing (Greg. Nyssa, *de infant*); juggling (Greg. Naz., *Orat.*, xxi.12).

Interested though they were in the structure and functions of the human body, the Greek fathers would not
have us think that this is all there is to be said about
man. Man is akin to the lower orders of creation not
only by virtue of possessing a body, but also in his
possession of a soul. The tripartite nature of soul, understood as intuitive, perceptive and rational, is almost a
commonplace in patristic writing, and it is this which
at the same time links man to the animal and lifts him
above it.[1] The very fact of bodily movement indicates
the presence of soul, writes Theophilus, and this much
man shares with animals.[2] It is here that the Greek
fathers show some independence of the Platonic tradition which in other respects and to varying degrees
influenced them.[3] It is no part of our purpose here to
follow the ramifications of Platonism through the centuries after Plato himself, which, both for itself and in
relation to patristic writings, has been the subject of
frequent study. In very general terms the Platonic tradition envisaged the soul of man as a purely spiritual
entity, uncreated and eternal, which enters the human
body either in obedience to universal cosmic law or
through its decline from its original destiny.[4] There is
no true harmony between body and soul, the body con-

[1] Clem. Alex., *Paed.*, iii.1; Origen, *de princ.*, ii.8.1; Greg. Nyssa.,
de hom. opif., viii.4–8; Basil, *Hex.*, viii.1.165b; Nemesius, *de. nat.
hom.*, i.2.

[2] *ad Autol.*, i.5.

[3] The ground is covered in detail by R. Arnou, 'Platonisme des
Pères' in *Dict. de Théol. catholique*, xii.2258–392.

[4] These views receive their classic statement in Plato, *Republic*,
10.611b; *Timaeus*, 41d; *Phaedrus*, 246ff; *Phaedo*, 246c.

stituting a tomb or prison from which it is the object of
the soul to be freed. The judgment myth towards the
end of the *Gorgias* depicts the soul of man appearing
before the judge stripped of its body; the entity to be
judged, the real man, is the soul.[1] In the *Phaedo* death
is shown as the release of the soul from the body, the
moment at which the soul achieves its proper independence, which is the aim of philosophy. The body is
cared for only as much as is needful to enable it to serve
the soul. The philosopher devotes his most careful attention to the soul.[2] The body is gross, untrustworthy and
obtrusive, and detachment from it is to be cultivated as
a preparation for death which will bring deliverance
from it.[3] In the *Timaeus* a balance between body and
soul is regarded as desirable since each affects the other
and can endanger it. The body must be exercised by
muscular action, and only in extreme cases subjected to
drugs.[4] The relation of soul to body is expressed by
Plato in a series of metaphors: the soul is the steersman
of the body, the charioteer driving the body which is its
vehicle; soul and body are interwoven.[5] Yet however
close the metaphors seek to link soul and body, they
remain distinct entities whose destiny is to be separated, a release for the soul rendered possible by the
degree to which in this present life it turns away from
the sensible and towards the intelligible and rational
realm of pure spirit. There is a real dualism here,
which subsequent centuries accentuated rather than
diminished.

It would be idle to pretend that Platonic denigration
of the body left no mark upon Christian thinking. There
runs through patristic writings a universal demand for
the strictest control of the body, sometimes for treatment

[1] So in *Euthydemus*, 278e–282d; 288a–292e.
[2] *Phaedo*, 64c–65a. [3] ibid., 66c–68b.
[4] *Timaeus*, 87c–89d.
[5] *Critias*, 109c; *Phaedrus*, 246a; *Timaeus*, 69c, 36e.

harsher than mere control. But in the considerable body
of Greek patristic writings we seldom find denigration
of the body and its functions. On the contrary, the body
is accorded a status which is quite foreign to that given
it by Plato himself or by Platonist writers after him.
Irenaeus writes:

By the hands of the Father, that is, by the Son and the Holy
Spirit, man, and not merely a part of man, was made in the
likeness of God. Now the soul and the spirit are certainly
part of the man, but certainly do not constitute the whole
of the man; for the complete man consists in the mingling
and union of the soul, which receives the spirit of the Father,
combined with that fleshly nature which was moulded after
the image of God. . . . For if any one should take away the
substance of the flesh (that is, of the handiwork of God) and
understand that which is purely spiritual, such then would
not be a spiritual man, but the spirit of a man. . . . For that
flesh which has been moulded is not in itself a complete man,
but is the body of a man, part of a man. Neither is the soul,
considered a part by itself, the man, but is the soul of a man,
part of a man. Neither is the spirit a man, for it is the spirit
and not man. The complete man is constituted of the
mingling and union of all three.[1]

This is part of a long passage in which Irenaeus con-
demns gnostic denigration of the body and seeks to
estimate the body at its proper worth. Clement of
Alexandria, for all his severe moral demands, insists that
God is the creator of man's body, 'flesh, marrow, bones,
nerves, veins, blood, skin, eyes, *pneuma*, righteousness,
immortality'.[2] Origen, noting the interaction of body
and mind, says that the nausea experienced by the body
at sea renders the mind dull, just as bodily fever renders
it dull on land, 'for we human beings are animals composed of a union of body and soul, and in this way alone
is it possible for us to live on earth'.[3] Athenagoras insists

[1] *adv. haer.*, v.6.1.   [2] *Protrept.*, x.98.2.3.
[3] *de princ.*, i.1.6.; cf. Eusebius, *Prae. evang.*, vi.6.

upon the union of body and soul to make a whole man, the mingling of the two constituents making 'one living being'.[1] Theodoret is disturbed by Plato's idea that the soul is entombed in the body, and puts against it Plato's own words from the *Republic* to the effect that since the soul can only live well because of its inhabiting of the body, the body must therefore be cared for.[2]

The emphasis upon the wholeness of man consisting in the union of body and soul receives its most forceful and consistent expression in the unanimity of the Greek fathers on the resurrection of the body. The fact that this article of belief gives rise to some strange analogies and observations of fancy need not distract us from the central point that is being made by the writers, that the concept of a whole man includes more than purely spiritual elements. Some of the fathers are troubled by the case of the bodily resurrection of a man whose body has been eaten or dispersed. Athenagoras attempts to overcome this difficulty physiologically. If an animal eats a human body, not all of the body is absorbed by the animal's tissues; it evacuates part of what it has eaten before the process of digestion has begun. Similarly, food that is unnatural to the eater is not absorbed by the tissues, so that not all that is eaten by cannibals is wholly destroyed.[3] Gregory of Nyssa propounds much the same question, referring to the body of a man eaten by fish after drowning, and adding the further refinement that the same fish might then be caught and eaten by other men. At first Gregory is content to leave the solution of the matter in God's hands, but a little later he adds that just as a common herd of cattle can be divided among its several owners, so the soul will be able to attract its scattered bodily elements, wherever they may be.[4]

[1] *de res. mort.*, xv.
[2] *Graec. affect. cur.,*. v13.14.
[3] *de res. mort.*, v; viii.
[4] *de hom. opif.*, xxv..1f; xxvii.2.

Bodies are in any case consumed by worms, writes
Cyril of Jerusalem, which makes this a question which
applies not in a few special cases only, but in all.[1]
Whatever changes the human body undergoes before
death, the risen body bears with it its own tokens of
identity.[2] Human bodies are subject to change, writes
Athenagoras, being affected by toil, worry, grief or
disease, overheating or chilling, or unsuitable food;[3] a
point he carries further in a later passage in which he
says that all future states are pre-figured in prior states.
Human semen, for example, is homogeneous in texture
but contains within itself such different textures as
bone, nerve, cartilage, muscle, flesh, intestine. Change,
he concludes, is a necessary concomitant of life,[4] pointing towards Paul's contrast in I Corinthians between
the earthly body and the risen body. This point is taken
up by Origen, who warns against the ease with which
it can be assumed that the 'risen body' is identical with
the earthly body. Transference of names of parts of the
body to the soul, and the use of the terms 'food' and
'drink' of the soul, have led, he says, to much nonsense,
such as that in the risen life bodily food and drink are
consumed.[5] He maintains that the Stoic doctrine of
cyclical conflagration and rebirth, though akin to a
doctrine of the resurrection of the body, commits the
same error, since it postulates the rebirth of a new body
which is identical with the old, whereas Christians hold
that the risen body is not in all respects identical with
the earthly, and that once risen it is incorruptible.[6] The
soul has need of a body suited to the nature of the

---

[1] *Cat.*, xviii.2f.

[2] Greg. Nyssa, *de hom. opif.*, xxvii.3f.

[3] *de res. mort.*, vii.

[4] ibid., xvii; so ps.-Justin, *de res.*, v.

[5] *Comm. in Cant.*, prol. ii. This is in essence the objection of
Dionysius of Alex. to the conception of the messianic kingdom
held by Nepos, *apud.* Euseb., *Hist. Eccles.*, vii.24.5.

[6] *c. Cels.*, v.20–3.

place it occupies,[1] and in its risen state has no need of a material body.[2] In case this should open him to the charge that he is making the risen body a wholly different entity from the earthly body, a different 'vehicle' in the Platonic sense, he makes use of an analogy which is probably common to every patristic writer, that of the plant rising from a seed, an analogy which maintains the principle of difference of structure to suit different conditions and at the same time maintains the principle of continuity.[3] It is significant that when Synesius of Cyrene, a kindly-disposed pagan philosopher, was offered the bishopric of Ptolemais in 410, the frank letter he wrote to his brother asserting his doctrinal position makes very plain that as a Platonist he is not prepared to abandon his belief in the immortality of the soul in favour of the Christian doctrine of bodily resurrection.[4] It says much for his high repute that his patriarch did not regard this as an insurmountable obstacle to his consecration.

If there is any true continuity between the earthly and the risen bodies, then matter, of which the former is composed, cannot be intrinsically evil. It is probable that Plato himself had not regarded the matter in this light. In the *Timaeus*, uncreated primordial matter exists solely in order to receive the impress of forms imposed upon it by mind, and in itself is neither bad nor good.[5] In the *Laws* evil seems to be attributed not to matter but to the soul.[6] But the later manifestations of Platonism, merged in varying degrees with other elements,

[1] The fixed stars are the abode of risen bodies, *de princ.*, ii.3.7.

[2] *c. Cels.*, vii.32f.

[3] ibid., v.17f; so Clem. Rom., *ad Cor.*, xxiv.3–5; Theophilus, *ad. Autol.*, i.13; Cyril of Jerus., *Cat.*, xviii.6; etc. The same point is common to the Latins, e.g. Tertullian, *de res.*, xii; Lactantius, *div. inst.*, vii.4; etc.

[4] *Ep.*, 105, *P.G.*, 66.1485b.

[5] *Timaeus*, 48e.

[6] *Laws*, 896e–898d.

gnostic, orphic, apocalyptic, came to regard matter un-
equivocally as evil. In the systems of the gnostic writers
the creation of matter was separated from God as far as
hierarchies of subsidiary spiritual beings could separate
it.[1] Marcion, gnostic in some respects, relegates the
creation of matter to the second and inferior God, the
record of whose works he was at such pains to expunge
from the scriptures. The same low view of the material
world runs through the work of Philo, for whom the
body is the 'polluted prison' of the soul, enjoying no
resurrection,[2] and it can be found in the work of
Plotinus.[3] The apocalyptic writings of the first century
A.D., especially those associated with Alexandria, share
the same standpoint, displaying a progressive withdrawal of messianic hopes from this world, culminating
in the plain attribution of evil to matter and in denial
of resurrection to the body.[4] It is in such a context of
dualistic pessimism that the Greek fathers assert the
resurrection of the body and deny the evil of matter.[5]

One aspect of their attitude towards the body is seen
in their opposition to the Docetic tendencies which
frequently threatened what they held to be the truth
about Jesus Christ. Early in the second century Ignatius
takes his stand against Docetic christology in his letters,
asserting to the Trallians, the Ephesians and the
Smyrnaeans the reality of Christ's incarnation and
death. 'If, as is said by some that are without God, that

[1] e.g. Irenaeus, *adv. haer.*, i.24.4 on Basilides; i.25.1 on Carpo-
crates.

[2] *Migr. abr.*, ii; *quod deus immut.*, xxxii.

[3] *Enn.*, i.8.3.

[4] e.g. *The Assumption of Moses*; *Wisdom*; *iv. Maccabees*. R. H.
Charles, *A Critical History of the Doctrine of a Future Life*, 2nd ed.,
London 1913.

[5] Harnack sees Christian teaching on food, drink and marriage
in early centuries as conscious opposition to Manichee dualism,
Medicinisches aus der ält. Kirchengeschichte, TU., viii.4, (Leipzig 1892),
p. 62.

is, the unbelieving, Christ became man in appearance only, that he did not in reality assume a body, that he died in appearance only and did not in fact suffer, then why am I now in bonds and long to face the wild beasts?' It is interesting that the matter should have been considered sufficiently pressing in the fourth century for the brief letters to be edited in a longer recension, the added material expanding the anti-docetic passages where they occur. At the end of the second century Serapion of Antioch, in a letter preserved by Eusebius, drew attention in no friendly spirit to the apocryphal Gospel of Peter, which showed Docetic leanings.[1] Emphasis upon the real manhood of Christ finds frequent expression in the work of Justin.[2] Irenaeus, too, constantly raises the same issue against the heretics: 'Christ performed his works not in appearance only but in actual reality . . . truly possessing flesh and blood.' 'Vain are the disciples of Valentinus who put forth this opinion, that they may exclude the flesh from salvation and cast away what God has fashioned.'[3] The point was put in formal manner, not for the intellectual satisfaction of the scholar but for the edification of the whole Church, in the words of the Nicene definition: 'And was made man, and was crucified also for us under Pontius Pilate. He suffered and was buried.' Human flesh, assumed by Christ, was not intrinsically evil. Pseudo-Justin writes of the dignity of the human body in God's sight.[4] 'The enemy is not the body, as some would have it', says Clement of Alexandria, 'but the devil.'[5] Those who denigrate created existence and vilify the body are lacking reason, not considering that the frame of man

[1] Euseb., *Hist. Eccles.*, vi.12.3–6.

[2] *Apol.*, i.21; 23; *Apol.*, ii.13; *Dial.*, xliii; xlviii; etc.

[3] *adv. haer.*, v.1.2; cf. iii passim; v.12.6, 'Why should Christ have healed human flesh if it were not to attain salvation?'

[4] *de res.*, vii.f.

[5] *Strom.*, iv.14.95.2.

F

was formed erect for the contemplation of heaven[1]—a point frequently made by the fathers. Origen defends the flesh from the imputation that it is intrinsically evil in provoking man to lust by arguing that the action of the body here is a purely physical matter, the eagerness of the body to empty passages which are filled with seminal fluid.[2] In itself, that is, the body is morally neutral. Against the distinction made by Celsus between the divinely-created soul and the body, which is purely animal and made by some other creator, Origen replies that Celsus can give no evidence for any other creator than God, and that the human body is not the same as an animal's body; bodies differ according to the soul within them.[3] Those who say that since Adam's body was formed before his soul, the body is nobler than the soul, writes Gregory of Nyssa, are as mistaken as those who say that the soul was in existence before the body. Soul and body alike come from God.[4] Cyril of Jerusalem says that it is not the body that must be blamed for sin; the soul leads the body into sin.[5] Whatever there is sinful in sexual relationships lies in the soul, not the body. God controls the physiological changes of the female body during pregnancy and birth, and these functions cannot therefore be evil.[6] We may recall the explanation given by Nemesius of the part played by the body in exciting lust: the testicles are stimulated by a pungent fluid flowing from the kidneys.[7] Throughout the lengthy treatment Nemesius gives to the bodily senses and their relation to the brain, there is no suggestion that the senses are dangerous to the soul. The matter is discussed with remarkable objectivity.[8] Chrysostom, expounding the Epistle to the Romans, argues that the superiority of the soul to the body (a point not disputed by the

[1] *Strom.*, iv.26.168.1.
[2] *de princ.*, iii.4.3.
[3] *c. Cels.*, iv.52–9.
[4] *de hom. opif.*, xxviii.1.
[5] *Cat.*, iv.23.
[6] *Cat.*, ix.15.
[7] *de nat. hom.*, xxviii.45.
[8] ibid., vii–xi.

fathers) does not imply that the body is therefore evil. The body is neither contrary to the soul nor opposed to it, he writes, but is to the soul as a harp is to a harpist, or a ship to a pilot, figures of speech which are reminiscent of Plato's charioteer. The soul leads, the body follows.[1] Paul does not disparage the flesh, writes Chrysostom of Romans viii. 5–7. So long as the body keeps its station and does not rise against the soul, all is well. The same point is made when Chrysostom reaches Romans viii. 12, 13, at which point he warns the reader against thinking that Paul is speaking against the flesh; Paul simply means that we should not let the flesh rule our life.

Man stands on the earth, and his erect posture enables him to look up to heaven.[2] This gives man unique importance in being at home in two worlds and linking them. Against the earlier Platonising tendency of Alexandria to regard man's rationality as a sharing of the divine mind by natural right, later theologians came to regard it rather as a reflection or image of divinity given to man as an act of grace by God.[3] The term 'image' called for careful and precise handling, as Eusebius found to his cost in controversy with Marcellus on the question of the relation of the Son to the Father within the Trinity. Eusebius had used the ill-defined term 'primary likeness' to elucidate the term 'image'.[4] But how can the eternal and transcendent have an

[1] *Comm. in Rom.*, xiii. (Rom. vii.17f).

[2] Theodoret, *de prov.*, iii, *P.G.*, 83.597b.

[3] e.g. Athanasius, *de incarn.*, iii. See A. Lieske, *Die Theologie der Logosmystik bei Origenes* (Münster 1938), pp. 120ff.

[4] *Dem. Ev.*, iv.2, *G.C.S.*, vi, p. 152. Cyril of Alex., like Euseb. more concerned with 'image' as applied to Christ rather than to man, was more careful to define the term closely, to show how different kinds of images reproduce their original in different ways, *Comm. in Joh.*, ii.373c–379a; cf. *de incarn.*, 686e–687a. Cyril's usage is discussed by W. J. Burghardt, *The Image of God in Man according to Cyril of Alex.* (Washington 1957).

image of any kind? In the sense, says Eusebius, in which
a statue of the emperor is an image of the emperor.[1] But
the statue is different from the emperor, and no talk of
'primary likeness' can establish their identity. Theodore
of Mopsuestia, treating of man as made in the image of
God, agrees with Marcellus. An image, he writes, while
itself seen, points to what is not seen, which is why
images are made in order to honour those who are
absent. Man is a reminder of the God who is not seen.[2]
This reminder works by analogy. Since man is in the
image of God, we can by observing man form some
conception of the greater sublimity of God. We do this
by subtracting from man all his points of weakness:
man, for example, encounters difficulties in creating,
whereas God creates from nothing at the moment of
willing to create; man becomes a father only by the aid
of woman and after the passage of time, whereas God
exists as Father from eternity without union with
another.[3] The image is a copy of the original,[4] and man,
as image, must remember that to God alone is real
existence and pure spirituality to be attributed.[5]

Man is also in part an image of the physical universe.
The conception of man as a microcosm goes back to the
Timaeus, where the cosmos is described as being com-
posed of body and soul,[6] and to the *Physics* of Aristotle,[7]

[1] *c. Marcell.*, i.4., *P.G.*, 24.764.

[2] *Comm. in Coloss.*, i.15.

[3] *Hom. cat.*, ii.16.

[4] ibid., xii.2. R. Devréesse (*Essai sur Théodore de Mopsueste*, Studi
e Testi 141 (Vatican City 1948), p. 13f) analyses Theodore's conception of man's likeness to God as consisting of (1) man's creator-
ship, (2) man's understanding, (3) man's ability to move in
thought throughout the cosmos, (4) man's ability to rule and
judge; cited by R. A. Norris, *Manhood and Christ* (Oxford 1963),
p. 141, who gives a careful survey of Theodore's position in
relation to the Platonism and Aristotelianism of his day.

[5] *Hom. cat.*, ix.11.

[6] Plato, *Timaeus*, 6.

[7] *Physics*, 252b, where the term 'microcosm' is first used.

and became an important element of Stoicism.[1] It
appears in patristic writings in Clement of Alexandria,
who writes of the 'new song' sung by the Word of God,
composing into melodious order the universe, and
especially man, who by virtue of being made of body
and soul is a universe in miniature.[2] For Origen the
human body, possessed like the physical universe by
daemons, constitutes a microcosm.[3] For Tatian the term
is applicable to man by reason of his control of a multi-
plicity of physical functions: eye, ear, hair, intestines,
the compacting together of marrow and bones and
sinews, all under a single control. Thus, says Tatian,
does the physical world also function.[4] Gregory of
Nyssa disagrees with pagan writers who say that man is
a microcosm composed of the same elements as the
universe: 'This is to dignify man with the attributes of
the gnat and the mouse, which are also composed of the
four elements.' In this sense man is not an image of the
universe.[5] But Gregory elsewhere modifies his view,
allowing that man can be termed a microcosm so long
as it is understood that the soul is in the image of God.[6]
He will also allow that man displays an order and
harmony similar to that which obtains in the universe:
it is reasonable, he writes, that in this respect the mind
should find in the microcosm what it finds in the
macrocosm.[7] Methodius also notes man's kinship with
the cosmos.[8] For Nemesius this is not matter for passing
observation, but is close to the heart of the argument of
his *de natura hominis*. Man, he says, enjoys life in common
with inanimate things—the faculties of nutriment and

[1] G. Bardy, *La vie spirituelle d'après le pères des trois premiers siècles*
(Paris 1935), p. 99.   [2] *Protrept.*, i.5.3.
[3] *Hom. in Jos.*, xxiv.1.   [4] *Orat. ad Graec.*, xii.
[5] *de hom. opif.*, xvi.1. This is the Stoic emphasis. Others would
have it that the universe was in the image of man.
[6] *de anim. et resurr.*, *P.G.*, 46.28b.
[7] *in psalm.*, i.3. *P.G.*, 44.441cd.
[8] *de res.*, ii.10.2.

generation in common with plants, voluntary movement and certain appetites in common with irrational
animals, reason and understanding and judgment with
the rational intelligences. Man therefore stands on the
boundary between the intelligible order and the phenomenal, occupying the central position of a single creation.[1] This was not quite the Stoic conception of unity.
W. Telfer shows that although Nemesius' view can
ultimately be traced back to Posidonius of Apamea,
Nemesius, like Gregory of Nyssa, saw creation as being
composed of two systems, the rational and the phenomenal, linked by man, rather than as a single system
including gods at one end and matter at the other, with
man as one element in the whole.[2] To Nemesius man
was more important than he could have been to
Posidonius, since it was man's function to hold together
the two orders of creation.[3] His importance Nemesius
saw to lie in his ability to incline in either direction,
towards the rational or towards the phenomenal, and
his consequent capacity for losing touch with the one if
he inclines too far towards the other. He cannot lose his
body by inclining towards the rational, but he can lose
his spiritual status by inclining too far towards the
phenomenal, thus breaking the unity which it is his
function to preserve and forfeiting his position as its
bond.[4] Nemesius returns to the point: as possessor of a
physical body man is the last-created of the phenomenal order, summing up that whole order in himself,
and therefore being called a microcosm. But as rational
being, man is navigator, astronomer, fisherman and
huntsman; is skilled in knowledge, arts and sciences; he

[1] *de nat. hom.*, i.2.

[2] *On the Nature of Man*, Lib. of Christian Classics iv, ed. William
Telfer (London 1955), p. 230f.

[3] A Platonising of the Stoic view which Telfer attributes to
Origen, *Comm. in Gen.*, with other possible intermediary sources in
addition.

[4] *de nat. hom.*, i.4.

writes, and thus communicates with people far away from him; he foretells the future; he rules, subdues, enjoys everything; he converses with angels and with God; he controls daemons.[1] Nemesius then continues through the greater part of his work to demonstrate the close connection between the physical and the psychical within man.[2]

Man, standing between two worlds and belonging to both at once, is in a position to estimate the phenomenal from the standpoint of the rational. This is not to say that he can see the physical universe through the eyes of God, for that vision he has forfeited. To see with the eyes of God was the prerogative of Christ alone, part of whose mission the fathers saw to be the filling of the link-position vacated by man in consequence of his sin. To the extent to which man is assimilated to the mind of Christ, he can interpret nature in the light of God's purpose, and can understand it correctly.

[1] ibid., i.10; cf. Eusebius' strikingly similar statement of man's superiority to the irrational order, *Theoph.*, i.49–67.

[2] e.g. *de nat. hom.*, xxvii.43, where Nemesius discusses bodily functions which are in part voluntary, in part involuntary; xxviii.45, where he indicates the bearing of physiology on ethics.

If it is true that the Greek fathers displayed deep interest in the natural world, it is equally true that they enjoyed it. This is sometimes obscured by their naturally austere cast of mind, and it is seldom that we find them enjoying themselves sensuously as though they were cats sleeping in the sun. Yet even so austere a figure as Origen, engaged upon probing the spiritual interpretation of a biblical text referring to an apple, cannot wholly avoid the sensuous. Wisdom, he writes, 'not only mixes her wine in the bowl; she also supplies fragrant apples in plenty, so sweet that they not only yield their luscious taste to mouth and lips but keep their sweetness also when they reach the inner throat'.[1] Where Origen leads, others will follow. What we do not find is an unhealthy licking of the lips over pleasures of sense that are denied, a sour relishing on paper of forbidden delights. There is warning in abundance against the dangers inherent in such pleasures, in particular, perhaps, those associated with taste,[2] but where enjoyment is permitted, the fathers enjoy to the full. A man who had endured the rigours of a Cappadocian winter would be less than human if he were insensitive to the spring which followed.

It is in their comments upon the seasons of the year that the Greek fathers often make their readers feel that they are writing from their own experience and are no

[1] *Comm. in Cant.*, iii.5; cf.iii.8; *Hom. ii in Cant.*, vi; Greg. Nyssa, *c. Eunom.*, ii.12; *de hom. opif.*, xxx.27.

[2] Basil, *ad nean.*, ix; cf. Greg. Nyssa, *de virg.*, xxi, 'above all be specially watchful against the pleasures of taste, for that seems in a way the most deeply rooted, and to be the mother, as it were, of all forbidden enjoyment'.

longer dependent upon literary sources. It is the eye of
a countryman which leads Basil to note, as a sign of
returning spring, the restless movement of the cattle in
their stalls.[1] Spring was eagerly awaited,[2] and was very
sweet when its first signs appeared—the sun gently
warming the frozen surface of the earth, buds half hidden beneath the soil, new grass, the return of the first
migrant birds—tokens, says Gregory of Nyssa, signs of
spring rather than spring itself.[3] Gregory of Nazianzus
has noted creatures thawing out in the new warmth, and
taking courage from the springtime, creeping out of
their burrows.[4] We find here too the age-old lament for
the shortness of spring. But at least there is another
spring to look forward to, for the flowers wither and
again revive, and after another shedding are again in
leaf, whereas nature exhibits the human bloom only in
the spring of early life and then kills it. It vanishes in
the frosts of age.[5] To the request of Nicobulus that
Gregory of Nazianzus should publish a collection of his
letters, Gregory replies that this is asking flowers from
an autumn meadow. Yet he consents.[6] Of winter they
find little good to say. Cyril of Jerusalem's eye wanders
to the window as he addresses his flock: 'The season is
winter, as you see; the trees now stand as though they
were dead.'[7] Basil envies the migrating cranes as winter
approaches,[8] and then takes to his house, snowed up,

---

[1] *Hex.*, ix.3.193b. This piece of observation is the more striking
from its irrelevance to Basil's argument. His point is the solicitude
of the Creator for his creatures, and he gives three brief examples:
the sheep eating greedily to prepare themselves for winter; the
cattle being restless before spring; the hedgehog making two air
vents to its hole. On the last point cf. Aristotle, *Hist. An.*, ix.6.612b.

[2] Basil, *Ep.*, x; Cyril of Jerus., *Cat.*, xviii.7.

[3] *Ep.*, 9.   [4] *Ep.*, 72.

[5] Greg. Nyssa, *de virg.*, iv; cf. Greg. Naz., *Orat.*, xlii.19.

[6] *Ep.*, 52. Greg. Nyssa cites the beauty of early autumn fruit
and flowers as one of the wonders of nature (*de infant*).

[7] *Cat.*, xviii.7; so also iv.30.   [8] *Ep.*, 193.

with all roads closed till the following Easter.[1] In the
Cappadocian winter all outdoor life came to a stand-
still,[2] but there were compensations. Things return in
their season, writes Basil to Olympus; in the spring the
flowers, in summer the corn, in autumn the apples, in
winter——? Winter's fruit is conversation.[3] Gregory of
Nyssa gives us a charming glimpse of the father of
Eunomius, 'one of those farmers who are always bent
over the plough and who spend a world of trouble on
their little farm; and in winter, when he was released
from working in the fields, he used to carve out neatly
the letters of the alphabet for boys to form syllables
with, winning his bread with the money these sold for'[4]
—an almost Wordsworthian picture of the simple
countryman.

Clement of Alexandria does not compose work
specifically about the natural world, and it is interesting
to observe how often natural references occur in his
works at moments when he is, as it were, off his guard,
thinking about something else. Clement is justly regarded as an important literary figure in the history of
Christianity, but his writing does not stray far from his
own soil even when his net is being cast wide among the
cultures and religions of the Mediterranean and the
Near East. He knows the shrewd expertise of the cook
and the shepherd inspecting a sheep, the one looking
for fat, the other for purity of breed;[5] and that of a
farmer looking at a vine with the eye of a specialist, and
of a horseman gauging the quality of a horse.[6] He
knows the feel of a hard-mouthed and powerful horse
that has taken the bit between his teeth,[7] and has seen

[1] *Ep.*, 198.

[2] Basil, *Epp.*, 48; 197; 350; 365.

[3] *Ep.*, 13.   [4] *c. Eunom.*, i.6.

[5] *Strom.*, i.1.17.1.   [6] ibid., i.6.34.2.

[7] *Quis dives*, xlii.6; cf. Greg. Naz., *Orat.*, xlv.12, who shows a hot-
tempered horse past its first youth needing coaxing before it will
take the bit in its mouth.

a horse come to its master's whistle.[1] The countryman
is to be discerned in Clement's image of a man falling
into a ditch that he had not seen or that was too wide
to be jumped,[2] and in his picture of men coaxing cattle
into a yard by holding out branches to entice them.[3]
He writes of the need for proper irrigation of land,[4] and
for keeping wells pumped out in order to maintain the
purity of the water.[5] He notes the tremendous growth of
green things after rain, springing from cultivated land
and dunghill alike, wheat and weeds, and trees sprouting from sepulchres;[6] the farmers clearing the ground
of weed before sowing;[7] pruning and thinning out the
growth of the vines.[8] He illustrates one point by referring to the sun shining through a chink in a window into
dark corners;[9] another by contrasting the blazing sun
by day and the 'borrowed light' of a lamp by night;[10]
another by a spark kindled by the rays of the sun
focused through a glass vessel full of water.[11] He gives us
glimpses of wool-dyeing, with the wool receiving its
proper treatment before the dyeing is begun;[12] of picking
almonds and finding the shells empty.[13] Most of these
examples occur in Clement's *Stromateis*. If the same
examples had occurred in the New Testament Gospels,
preachers would never tire of extolling our Lord's
wonderful intimacy with nature. H.-I. Marrou draws
attention to the sheer erudition which Clement displays
in the *Paedagogos*.[14] This extends to everything he wrote.

[1] *Protrept.*, x.92.1.
[2] *Strom.*, ii.15.62.3.   [3] ibid., ii.20.111.3.
[4] ibid., i.1.17.4.   [5] ibid., i.1.12.2.
[6] ibid., i.7.37.1.
[7] ibid., i.1.15.2.
[8] ibid., i.9.43.1; vi.8.65.5; *Paed.*, i.5.21.2.
[9] *Strom.*, vii.3.21.7.   [10] ibid., v.5.29.5f.
[11] ibid., vi.17.149.1.
[12] ibid., i.9.78.1.
[13] ibid., vii.16.99.5.
[14] *Sources chrétiennes* 70 (Paris 1960), Introd., p. 75.

His interests include the conception and growth of the
foetus; lactation; the growth of children; intoxication;
drugs abstracted from plants; sheep; female anatomy;
the physiological changes in birds during spring; bodily
exercise. Much of this we have noticed in greater detail
in an earlier chapter. But his references to small details
of country life, especially in the *Stromateis*, reveal not so
much the erudition of a learned man, as the knowledge
of a man who observed closely and appreciated what he
observed. 'He gives you . . . the vast earth to till,'
writes Clement in the *Protrepticos*, 'water to drink and
to sail on, air to breathe, fire to work for you, a world to
dwell in.'[1] Again, indulgence of the passions accom-
panied by pleasure is a dangerous poison, yet at the
same time 'a boon so great, the greatest ever given by
God to the human race'.[2] Clement's stern moral demands need no emphasis. The point here is that these
demands did not spring from fear or hatred of the
natural world. The combination of moral sternness and
appreciation of the whole immense stretch of nature
from the heavens above to the empty almond shell in
the grass, has in it something of the quality of Tertullian,
who also, for all his moral fierceness, will never allow
us for a moment to scorn the world we live in, but
sweeps us from the thunders and lightnings[3] to 'a single
tiny flower from any hedgerow . . . a single shellfish
from any sea, . . . a single stray wing of a moorfowl'.[4]
The bite of Tertullian's prose makes better reading
than Clement's, but they stand together in their appreciation of nature.

Origen presents a different picture. His eyes are in
long focus, and if his vision passes over the almond nut

---

[1] *Protrept.*, xi.115.1.   [2] ibid., x.99.2f.

[3] *ad scap.*, iii.

[4] adv. Marc., i.13; cf. i.14. For Tertullian's resolute defence of
the wonder and sanctity of the human body, see *ad uxorem* (passim);
de carn. Christi, iv; *de res. carnis*, ivf.

and the moorfowl's wing it is not because he does not regard them as works of God, each beautiful in its way. He is, when occasion demands, as ready as Clement to write of irrigation,[1] the dependence of farm work upon the seasons,[2] the bite of the mosquito,[3] or the cultivation of vines;[4] but occasion demands it less often than with Clement. Origen, moreover, does not illustrate his points in the discursive manner of Clement. For example, the usual practice of the fathers in presenting the doctrine of the resurrection of the body is to demonstrate by illustration that it is found in various guises throughout creation, in the return of seasons, the growth of crops and plants, the cycles of the planets and of sun and moon. Origen illustrates the same point by reference to the scriptures and what may be inferred from them. There is, however, a range of natural imagery which recurs constantly with Origen—the sun and moon, light and darkness, heat and fire, lightning.[5] This is to be attributed partly to Origen's concern with cosmological questions, but the impression it gives is that we are in the presence of the eagle, looking steadily and unblinkingly into the heart of the sun.[6] Gregory of

---

[1] *c. Cels.*, iv.44; reminding us that problems of irrigation were never far from man's mind in Egypt in the third century as in the twentieth.

[2] ibid., iv.79.   [3] *Hom. in Exod.*, iv.6.

[4] ibid., vi.10.

[5] Sun and moon: *de princ.*, praef. 10; i.1.5f; i.7.2; iii.1.11; *c. Cels.*, v.6, 7, 10; *Comm. in Rom.*, vii.4. Stars and planets: *de princ.*, i.7.3, 5; ii.3.6f; ii.11.5; xxv.4; *c. Cels.*, i.58f; v.21; viii.52. Light and darkness: *de princ.*, i.2.7; *c. Cels.*, ii.67; vi.5, 60; *Hom. in Exod.*, v.4. Heat and fire: *de princ.*, ii.6.6; ii.8.3; iii.1.11. Lightning: *de princ.*, i.5.5; *c. Cels.*, iv.75.

[6] This may not be unconnected with Origen's reputed mysticism. 'The fact is that Origen's theology of the spiritual life takes no account of the part played by darkness in the life of the soul; it deals only with light. . . . It is a speculative theory of the way the mind is illuminated by the gnosis . . .' J. Daniélou, *Origen* (English tr., London and New York 1955), p. 297.

Nyssa, who refers to heavenly bodies and to the effect
of light and heat perhaps as often as does Origen,
remains a more human figure, a man who is interested
by the structure of earthly things and touched by their
beauty. Occasionally, it is true, we are blinded by trying
to follow his direct vision,[1] but on very many occasions
our attention is distracted from the radiance itself by
some point of scientific interest,[2] or of beauty,[3] or the
wording leads the mind away from the heat and the
light to some object more grateful to the eye.[4] Origen's
sunbeams lead the eye and the mind upward to the
heart of light; Gregory's sunbeams, despite his Origen-
ism and his mysticism, despite his Platonic language
about beautiful objects being the ladder by which one
climbs to the intellectual beauty,[5] come down to be
played with by children at the window.[6] When we read
Gregory's words about a farmer grasping in his hands a
fork in order to break up clods of earth,[7] or a badly-
matched pair of horses pulling unevenly in the shafts,[8]
or the centrifugal ripples on the surface of a pond after
a stone has been thrown into it,[9] we are back in the
familiar world of Clement of Alexandria. Gregory of
Nazianzus has the sensitive eye of an artist. Searching
for a natural analogy to the Trinity, he reaches the well-
worn idea of a ray from the sun disseminating light.

[1] c. Eunom., i.36.

[2] ibid., viii.1; de virg., xi; de infant, the function of eyelashes
in shielding eyes from light; de hom. opif., xxi.3; orat. cat. magn., v;
in hex., P.G., 44.66d., 76d; 77b; 93a.

[3] de virg., xi; de hom. opif., i.5.

[4] c. Eunom., i.28, 'Heat is inherent in fire, splendour in the sunbeam, fluidity in water, downward tendency in a stone.' ibid.,
iv.7, 'The heaven admits no comparison with the earth, with the
stars, nor the stars with the seas, nor water with stone, nor animals
with trees. . . .'

[5] de virg., xi.

[6] antirrhet. c. Eunom. (= c. Eunom., xiib).

[7] c. Eunom., i.27.   [8] de virg., xxii.

[9] ibid., xiv.

Unlike many of his fellows, he sees that this analogy
will not serve, but before discarding it he pauses to
describe it as few others have done: 'a ray of the sun
flashing upon a wall and trembling with the movement
of the moisture which the beam has taken up in mid-air,
and being checked by the hard surface has set up a
strange quivering'.[1] He too can note the homely, such
as a stick carried along unsteadily in the eddies of a
stream,[2] or the difficulty of parting two bullocks which
have shared the same manger and the same yoke,[3] or a
gardener accidentally breaking a crooked sapling that
he was trying to bend straight.[4] Theodoret, who leads
his reader through almost Eusebian wastes of cosmological speculation,[5] enlivens his account of Providence
by comparing the human body to a well-drained and
ventilated house,[6] or by a reference to a dog greeting its
master with lowered ears and wagging tail.[7] Athanasius,
who is not given to flights of fancy, captures in an early
work the alarm of a man who sees children teasing a
snake or a lion, before he realises that the beast is dead.[8]
Chrysostom notes the wind helping gardeners to pull
down a dead tree,[9] and a dove, frightened in its cage,
beating itself against the roof trying to escape.[10]

Perhaps the most remarkable piece of patristic appreciation of scenery is the letter written by Basil com-
mending to Gregory of Nazianzus the attractions of his
hermitage overlooking the River Iris.

There is a high mountain covered with a thick forest,
watered on its northerly side by cool and transparent

---

[1] *Orat.*, xxxi.31.   [2] *Ep.*, 81.
[3] *Orat.*, xlii.24.   [4] ibid., xlv.12.
[5] *Graec. affect. cur.*, iv; cf. Euseb., *Prae. Evang.*, xiv.
[6] *de prov.*, iii. *P.G.*, 83.596b-d.
[7] ibid., 597c.   [8] *de incarn.*, xxix.
[9] *de incomp.*, iii. *P.G.*, 48.719a.
[10] ibid., 727d.

streams. At its base is outstretched an evenly sloping plain, ever enriched by moisture from the mountain. A forest of many-coloured and multifarious trees, a spontaneous growth surrounding the place, acts almost as a hedge to enclose it, so that even Calypso's isle, which Homer seems to have admired above all others for itself, is insignificant in comparison with this. For it is, in fact, not far from being an island, since it is shut in on all sides by barriers. Two deep ravines break off abruptly on two sides, and on a third side, at the bottom of a cliff, the river which glides gently by forms a wall, being itself a continuous and impassable barrier; and since the mountain stretches along the fourth side, and is joined to the ravines through bending sides which take the form of a crescent, the passes at the base are blocked off. However, there is one entrance here, and we are in control of it. Adjoining my dwelling is another neck of land, as it were, which supports at its summit a lofty ridge, so that from the former the plain below lies outspread before the eyes, and from the elevation we may gaze upon the encircling river, which in my mind at least furnishes no less pleasure than they who receive their first impression of the Strymon from Amphipolis. For the latter, as it spreads out with its somewhat sluggish current to form the lake, almost ceases to be a river by reason of the stillness of its waters; whereas the former, as it flows more swiftly than any other river I know, for a short space is roughened by the rock which borders upon it. As the river recoils from the rock it coils itself into a deep whirlpool, furnishing me and every spectator with a most pleasant sight, and providing the natives of the region with complete independence in regard to food, since it nourishes in its eddies an innumerable multitude of fish. Why need I mention the exhalations from the land, or the breezes from the river? Someone else might well marvel at the multitudes of the flowers or of the song of birds; but I have not the leisure to turn my thoughts to these. The highest praise, however, which I can give to the place is that, although it is well adapted by its admirable situation to producing fruits of every kind, for me the most pleasing fruit it nourishes is tranquillity, not only because it is far removed from the disturbances of the city, but also because it attracts not even a wayfarer, except the guests who join me in hunting. For besides its other excellencies, it abounds in game, not those bears and wolves of yours; but it feeds herds of deer and wild goats, hares, and animals like these.[1]

This glowing account should be read in conjunction with Gregory's reply to it. Admiring what he calls Basil's mousehole, he writes:

All that has escaped the rocks is full of gullies, and whatever is not a gully is a thicket of thorns; and whatever is above the thorns is precipice; and the road above that is precipitous and slopes both ways, exercising the mind of travellers and calling for gymnastic exercise for safety. And the river rushes roaring down, which to you is a Strymon of Amphipolis for quietness, and there are not so many fishes in it as stones, nor does it flow into a lake but dashes into abysses, O my grandiloquent friend and inventor of new names!

And much more in the same vein.[2] Basil seems to have taken the jest well, for Gregory pursues the matter further in his next letter. 'How shall I pass over that garden which was no garden and had no vegetables, and the Augean dunghill which we cleared out of the house and with which we filled up the garden, when we drew that mountainous wagon with our necks and hands, which still bear the marks of our labours.'[3] But Gregory had enjoyed every minute of it. 'O that I could go back to those early days, when I luxuriated with you in hard living! . . . O for the gatherings of wood and the cuttings of stone! O for the golden plane tree under which we sat, which I planted, and Apollos—I mean your worthy self—watered!'[4]

[1] Basil, *Ep.*, xiv. The translation is that of Roy J. Deferrari, *Saint Basil, the Letters* (Loeb., ed., London and New York 1926–39. Vol. i, pp. 106–10). I have altered a few phrases.

[2] Greg. Naz., *Ep.*, iv.

[3] *Ep.*, v.   [4] *Ep.*, 6.

G

We may feel that Gregory's instinct to jest at Basil's fulsome account was justified, and probably no-one but a friend of so long standing would have dared to deflate Basil to his face—Basil was already ὁ μέγας. But was it only a jest? It is possible to see beneath it something of embarrassment, not at Basil's grandiloquence itself, but at the subject of it, for what is so remarkable about Basil's description of the scenery round his hermitage is precisely that he is singing the praises of scenery in its wild state. The classical and Christian education received by Basil and Gregory would have impressed upon them that scenery is to be admired when the ordering impress of man's hand is seen upon it. God planted a garden (παράδεισος) eastward in Eden as the culmination of his ordering of chaos. It was beautiful because it was ordered, and thus Gregory of Nyssa could write of it before man appeared in it, 'animals skipping about, running to and fro in the thickets, while every sheltered and shady spot was ringing with bird song'.[1] These thickets and shades were thought of not as wild, untamed places such as might delight the taste of later centuries, but part of God's planting. This was not the primeval jungle but Paradise, for the mind trained in Plato and Aristotle would see no beauty in disorder, any more than the mind trained in the Old Testament scriptures would see beauty in the wilderness, which was always conceived as hostile and dangerous to man. God planted; and man's work was to 'replenish and subdue'.[2] Beauty emerged when man carried out this work and set upon the raw material of nature the impress of his rational intelligence. Natural beauty is often praised by the Greek fathers, but it is almost invariably farmland, parkland, cultivated land.[3] A parallel to this is the

---

[1] de hom. opif., i.5.   [2] Gen., i.28.
[3] e.g. Clem. Alex., Strom., i.7.37ff; vi.1.2.1; vii.18.111.1f. Heresy is like good land gone back to nature, bearing a crop of weeds, thorns and wild trees; Chrysostom, de incomp., iii.

patristic view of rivers and streams, which up to a point can be controlled by man, and are therefore friendly and beautiful; and of the sea, which is untamable by man and therefore hostile. Minucius Felix's admiration of the calm sea as Octavius dug his toes into the sand at Ostia is rare.[1] More characteristic is Gregory of Nazianzus, 'I prefer to stay ashore and plough a short but pleasant furrow, saluting the sea from a respectful distance.'[2] But Basil's praise of his hillside breaks the tradition. Gregory of Nazianzus would have subscribed heartily to praise of the solitude; that was the purpose of their withdrawal to the Iris. But to praise scenery in its wild and unsubdued state was something new, and Gregory, unprepared for it, covers the breach of good taste by a little friendly mockery. We may observe that his mockery stops at the very point at which the human element is introduced into the picture, for a pastoral idyll is complete only with figures. When Basil and Gregory start working on their land, to Gregory it is then that Paradise appears under man's replenishing and subduing hand. But Basil had lavished praise upon the place itself before the work had started, and it is in this that the uniqueness of Basil's description lies.

In contrast with Basil's description of his hermitage is Gregory of Nyssa's account of the estate at Vanota, where 'the river Halys makes the place beautiful to look upon with its banks, and gleams like a golden ribbon through their deep purple, reddening his current with the soil he washes down. Above, a densely wooded mountain stretches with its long ridge covered at all points with the foliage of oaks.' But this is not what really excites Gregory. 'The natural growth of timber, as it comes down the hillside, meets at the foot the planting of men's husbandry.' It is this cultivated land which

[1] *Octav.*, iii.

[2] *Orat.*, ii.10. cf. Eusebius' treatment of rivers and the sea; refs. in my *Eusebius of Caesarea* (London 1960), p. 88f.

arouses his admiration to its highest pitch. He describes
the vines, looking particularly good at that time of year;
apples, pears, peaches and crossbred fruit of various
kinds; the shady walk between the vines, the rose
pergolas, the fish pond with fish coming to be fed from
man's hand; and the breakfast that was served there,
with its savoury dishes, sweetmeats, drinking of healths,
wine cups.[1] In his next letter Gregory seems hardly to
have shaken off the wonder of the place, for his praise
of poverty includes the phrase, 'poverty, that laudable
and desirable evil'.[2]

With these lyrical utterances we must associate the
splendid hymns written by Synesius of Cyrene, with
some little hesitation in so far as one is not quite sure
whether to regard him as one of the Christian fathers or
not.[3] These hymns, sometimes echoing the paradoxes of
the Hymn of Jesus in the apocryphal *Acts of John*,[4] have
a way also of echoing the Hebrew book of Psalms in
summoning all creation to the praise of its God. 'To
Thee all things offer endless praise: day and night,
lightnings, snows, the heavens and the aether, roots of
the earth, water, air, all embodied creatures, all spirits,
seeds and fruits, plants and grasses, roots and growing
things, beasts and birds and shoals of swimming fish.'[5]
'Under thy holy laws, O blessed one, the flocks of white
stars graze in the airy bowl of the boundless heavens.
Thy works thou dost perform among the heavenly
beings, the aetherial, the earthly and the infernal, and

[1] Greg. Nyssa, *Ep.*, xv.

[2] *Ep.*, xvi.

[3] Whether or not Theophilus, patriarch of Alexandria, had
serious doubts about consecrating Synesius, his Cyrenaican flock
had no doubts about electing him, and afterwards had no reason
to regret their choice. See H-I. Marrou, *Synesius of Cyrene and
Alexandrian Neoplatonism*, in *The Conflict between Paganism and Christianity in the Fourth Century*, ed. A. Momigliano (Oxford 1963).

[4] e.g. Synes., *hymn.*, iii.190ff.

[5] ibid., iii.341–56; cf. Ps. 148.

dost apportion to them their life.'[1] Perhaps the most beautiful is the second hymn of the ten, a hymn of praise to God at dawn: 'Again the light, again the dawn, again the day brightens after the shades of night.'[2] There is nothing quite like this anywhere else in the Greek fathers. Perhaps we are here on the fringe of something more ancient than the Christian Church, something nearer to nature than any of the fathers were willing to recognise in themselves, which Theophilus the patriarch recognised in Synesius and which made him pause before consecrating.

The beauty of the natural world the Greek fathers gratefully acknowledge; the beauty of the human form they recognise, but approve only with reservations concerning its moral implications; beauty of building and of the plastic arts they approve as an aid to worship; beauty of literary style they hardly approve at all.[3] This amounts not to an admission of insensitivity to beauty, but an admission that human beings may not be able to deal adequately with beauty when they are faced by it. Origen's ungrateful association of poetic inspiration with insanity[4] would have been perfectly intelligible to a Greek mind which drew the thinnest of lines between erotic love, religion and poetry, the poet being able to fan Dionysiac frenzy by the skilful use of popular myth. It was a dangerous area of human experience. Faced by beauty manifested in human figure, or in literature, painting and sculpture, a man was on the fringe of the irrational, to step over into which would be to endanger his human status, his full rationality. That Origen was only too well aware of human beauty emerges momentarily in passages such as his treatment of Canticles i. 13, where he contrasts the breasts of the chaste with those

[1] ibid., iv.170.   [2] ibid., ii.1–3.
[3] See Appendix, p. 95.
[4] de princ., iii.3.4.
[5] Hom. in Cant., ii.3.

of harlots.[1] That way madness lies, and Origen has not
gone entirely uncensored for his flight from it by way of
self-mutilation in early youth. It was not that beauty
was in itself evil, any more than the flesh was itself evil.
It was irrationality that was to be feared, as was manifest to Sophocles long before and Albertus Magnus long
after.[1] In the presence of the beauty of natural objects
the fathers could feel safe, but it is to be noted that
Chrysostom was not even certain of this. Beauty is to
be admired, he writes, in buildings, works of art, the
human body. But standing before the sea one is seized
not with admiration only, but with fear and vertigo.
Chrysostom does not pass over the point, for it is
important. He traces the stages of his experience at this
moment—astonishment, fear, stupor, vertigo. It is a
religious experience, for this is what the prophet experi-
ences.[2] Paul had been seized with it, he says, as though
standing before a limitless ocean.[3] Chrysostom is describing the awe of man in the presence of the *mysterium
tremendum*, when he is on the fringe not of the irrational
but of what is more awful, the utterly rational, the
divine. The beauty of the sea can lead a man outside
himself to apprehend the divine, just as the beauty of
a woman can lead a man outside himself to be aware
of his animal heritage. Nature, in short, has an importance beyond itself, which is not be be defined in terms
of mere prettiness or utility. Nature, as God's handiwork, is sacramental.

---

[1] Soph., *Antigone*, 683ff; Alb. Magn., *in Pet. Lomb. Sentent.*, iv,
dist., xxvi, art. 7.

[2] The mystic also, perhaps. We are here not far removed from
Origen's account of knowledge which stuns the mind, causing an
'astonishment' which is akin to 'sober intoxication'. (*Hom. in Num.*,
xxvii.12; *Comm. in Joh.*, i.30); cf. Gregory of Nyssa's 'divine and
sober intoxication' (*Hom. in Cant.*, x).

[3] *de incomp.*, i. *P.G.*, 48.705b; cf. Greg. Nyssa, *Hom. in Eccles.*,
viii., *P.G.*, 44.729d–732a.

Appendix: The Greek Fathers' attitude towards beauty in literature, painting and sculpture

Opposition to beauty of literary style, which is raised by Latins as well as Greeks, is very widespread.[1] In general the standpoint of the east is that of Augustine in the west, that a statement does not become more true because more beautifully said. That this is not identical with an attack upon pagan philosophy is made clear by Basil, who writes to Diodorus that the rich diction and figures of speech in a book which had been sent to him caused delay, wasted time and disrupted continuity of thought, whereas the best pagan philosophers, such as Aristotle and Theophrastus, dealt with facts only, lacking the literary grace of Plato.[2] The Pauline strictures upon the wisdom of this world are made by Chrysostom to apply here.

If I demanded the polish of Isocrates, and the grandeur of Demosthenes, and the dignity of Thucydides, and the sublimity of Plato, then it would be right to confront me with this testimony of Paul [II Corinthians xi.6]. But as it is, let those qualities pass, and the superfluous embellishments of pagan writers. I take no account of style or expression. Yea, let a man's style be poor and his diction simple and unadorned, but let him not be rude in the knowledge and careful statement of doctrine.[3]

Paul's only ornament, says Gregory of Nyssa, was truth; he disdains to lower his style to prettiness and teaches us to fix our attention on truth alone.[4] Variants of the theme of the unlettered simplicity of the style of the biblical authors occur frequently: Jesus chose simple men; the prophets and evangelists despised

---

[1] Jerome hankered on occasions for the beauties of classical Latin, *Epp.*, vii.1; x; xxii.30; cxxv.12. Tertullian, one of the severest critics of classicism, was ironically one of the best stylists.

[2] *Ep.*, 135.

[3] *de sacer.*, iv.6; cf. ii.7; iii.9.

[4] *c. Eunom.*, i.4.

elegance of style;[1] the prophets did not use artificial arguments, clever words, deceptive syllogistic reasoning, but simple straightforward teaching;[2] the apostles had no skill in fine talking.[3] Further, beauty of style can be dangerous: 'Stop your song, Homer! It is not beautiful. It teaches adultery,' cries Clement of Alexandria.[4] For Origen poetic inspiration is akin to possession by daemons in insanity,[5] and few have benefited from the beautiful and polished style of Plato.[6] The spiritually immature can be seriously harmed by secular studies.[7] Eloquence, says Theophilus, can conceal evil like honey concealing a harmful drug.[8] Therefore, runs the conclusion, be on your guard against eloquence;[9] it is the heretics who train themselves in rhetoric.[10] The fathers pride themselves on uncouthness of style, beginning a work with a kind of Socratic disclaimer, as does Irenaeus: 'You will not expect from me any display of rhetoric nor excellence of composition, which I have never practised, nor any beauty and persuasiveness of style, to which I have no pretensions.'[11] Gregory of Nazianzus, himself no mean rhetorician, saw some use in pagan letters, analogous to the beneficial drugs

[1] Origen, *c. Cels.*, iii.39; vii.60.

[2] Eusebius, *Dem. Evang.*, i.1.

[3] Theodoret, *Graec. affect. cur.*, praef. i. The whole of book i demonstrates how the Greek writers have now gone to school to the barbarians.

[4] *Protrept.*, iv.59.2.

[5] *de princ.*, iii.3.4.

[6] *c. Cels.*, vi.2.

[7] *Hom. in Num.*, xx.3. At their best, pagan letters are irrelevant, ibid., i.1.

[8] *ad Autol.*, ii.12. It is the contents, not the ornaments, that matter, ibid., i.1; cf. Minucius Felix, *Octav.*, xv, Truth, not style, should determine the outcome of an argument.

[9] Origen, *Hom. in Jesu Nave.*, vii.7.

[10] Basil, *Ep.*, 90.

[11] *adv. haer.*, i. praef., a work which is noted indeed for its confusion of construction.

which can be extracted from the venom of snakes,[1] and
approved Athanasius for studying pagan literature and
philosophy so that he might not be utterly ignorant
of what he had determined to despise.[2] Basil advises
young men to benefit from pagan letters as far as this
is possible; that is, to take from them whatever is of
spiritual benefit. Some people, he says, enjoy flowers
for their fragrance and colour, but the bees extract
honey as well. It is like picking a bloom from a rose bed
and avoiding the thorns,[3] an image which he uses
differently and more gracefully in a letter to Libanus
of Antioch: your letters, he writes, are delightful, yet
prickly with reproaches—but those who like roses are
not deterred by thorns.[4] It is worth noting that Libanus
held a high opinion of Basil's own literary ability, as did
Byzantine scholars during the succeeding centuries.[5]

Beauty of literary style was suspect: beauty in paint
or stone was approved or not in accordance with the
morality of the subject of the painting or carving.
Irenaeus shows some insight into the frustrations of
artistic creation in saying that though an idea comes
rapidly to an artist's mind, he can only execute it
slowly because of the lack of perfect pliability in his
material.[6] In addition, what a work of art can achieve
is at best limited: sculpture, says Theodoret, can imitate
the physical appearance of an animal or man, but not
its movement.[7] There is no suggestion that art can do
anything but imitate nature, in the sense in which
Plato expounded this idea,[8] rather than in Aristotle's
sense of art imitating things as they ought to be.[9] This

---

[1] *Orat.*, xlii.11.   [2] ibid., xxi.6.

[3] *ad nean.*, iv.   [4] *Ep.*, 342.

[5] J. M. Hussey, *The Church and Learning in the Byzantine Empire*
(Oxford 1937), p. 107.

[6] *adv. haer.*, ii.33.4.

[7] *de prov.*, iii., *P.G.*, 83.592c.

[8] *Republic*, x.597e.

[9] *Poetics*, xxv.1.

is implicit in much of what Clement says about painting; that by the use of perspective it gives the illusion,
on a flat surface, of a scene in depth;[1] that it is not possible to copy with perfect accuracy the outward appear-
ances of things,[2] still less spiritual realities, since the
illusion is limited by the observer's consciousness of the
materials used by the artist.[3] Paintings can go far to
create illusion, but not to the extent of deceiving a
rational being.[4] Origen too contrasts the beauty of real
flesh in a living body with the painting on a canvas.[5]
The painted image of a person can never achieve closer
likeness to its original than an image reflected in a
mirror.[6] Clement could cite scriptural justification for
believing that artists—musician, potter, singer, per-
former, engraver of seals—are inspired by God,[7] but
they are not truly creators, only reshapers of material
already created by God.[8] A work of art must in any
case be judged by its moral content, whether painting
or music; either can be decorous or licentious.[9] Clement
will therefore not countenance the verse of Homer, or
pictures representing Aphrodite, or rings carved with
Leda and the swan.[10] Origen, who censures those who
fix their gaze on the evil handiwork of moulders and
sculptors,[11] nevertheless recognises that some sculptors
are very proficient in their art; he mentions the
Olympian Juppiter of Pheidias as especially good.[12]
Basil sees no deep or lasting significance in art, in so far
as the works of art will disappear with this world,[13] but

---

[1] *Strom.*, i.4.25.4.   [2] ibid., vi.18.164.1.
[3] ibid., vi.5.28; vi.6.   [4] *Protrept.*, iv.57.3f.
[5] *Hom. in Exod.*, vi.5.
[6] Greg. Nyssa., *c. Eunom.*, ii.12; cf. *de virg.*, xxiii.
[7] *Strom.*, i.4.25.4.   [8] ibid., vi.16.147.3.
[9] ibid., vi.16.150.5.   [10] *Protrept.*, iv.59.2–60.2.
[11] *c. Cels.*, vi.66.
[12] ibid., viii.17.
[13] *Ep.*, 277. Having said in a letter to Theodorus (*Ep.*, 124) that
he has heard that a lover, parted from his love, can check the

admits the didactic value of mural paintings: what the language of history teaches by the ear, mute design shows by imitation.[1] This is expanded by Gregory of Nyssa, who praises a painted mosaic scene in the chapel dedicated to the martyr Theodore: 'the artist has depicted all this by the art of colours, as in a book which possesses a tongue. For mute design is able to speak from the walls upon which it stands, and renders a very great service.'[2] Beauty in buildings was perfectly acceptable to Chrysostom,[3] as to Gregory of Nyssa and Eusebius, though in the case of Gregory's praise of the buildings at Vanota and Eusebius' of the great ecclesiastical foundations of Constantine and Helena, there is more than a suspicion that beauty is equated with mere richness and size.[4]

In all this there is little evidence of interest in art in any respect other than its conduciveness to good morality and its ability to instruct. The fathers were probably hampered in their aesthetic appreciation by the Mosaic censure of graven images, and by the fact that for three centuries after Christ there was no development of a distinctively Christian iconography. Christian art used the pictorial conventions of pagan artists, and did so at times with uneasiness of mind.[5]

---

violence of his passion through looking at a picture of his beloved, Basil adds, 'whether this is true I cannot say'.

[1] *Hom.*, xix, *in sanctos quad. mart.*

[2] *de laud. Theod.*

[3] *de incomp.*, i., *P.G.*, 48.705b.

[4] Euseb., *de vita Const.*, i.42; iii.25–40; iii.41ff; iii.48ff; iii.51ff; iii.58.

[5] Celsus reproves Christians for refusing to carve representations of their God, *apud* Origen, *c. Cels.*, vii.62. The Christians were embarrassed by the close association of sculpture and idolatry. See *The Church in the Roman Empire*, ii, J. R. Palanque, G. Bardy, P. de Labriolle, G. de Plinval, Louis Bréhier (London 1932), pp. 589–99.

There is no uneasiness discernible in Clement's development of the Christ–Orpheus theme in the *Protrepticos*, a theme which appears a century later in two decorations in the Roman catacomb of Domitilla, though Clement specifically repudiates pagan animal myths and associates the song which tames men, the most intractable of animals, with the 'new song' of Isaiah xlii.10 and Psalm 149.[1]

[1] *Protrept.*, i.1.1–6.5. See Pierre du Bourguet, S.J., *Early Christian Painting* (London 1965), p. 16.

Chrysostom's experience of vertigo as he stood on the sea shore led him to believe that nature has a significance and a meaning beyond what is immediately apparent, a significance which may be apprehended, as Chrysostom apprehended it, with frightening emotional intensity but vague definition, as a sudden awareness of the divine. The experience can then be subjected to reasoned analysis, a process which leads the fathers to the conclusion that nature is an ordered system from which must be inferred an ordering mind, namely God. It must be recognised, of course, that because a writer refers frequently to natural phenomena it does not follow that therefore he sees in them significance and meaning. This may be illustrated in parentheses by reference to two non-Christian writers of the second century, Lucian and Marcus Aurelius. Lucian's brilliance in describing characters and scenes, matched among the fathers perhaps only by Tertullian, does not concern us here. We are concerned with his natural references, which occur constantly. In *Demonax* he refers to the location of the antipodes, the weight of smoke resulting from burning a thousand pounds' weight of wood, and the discoloration on the leg of an old man.[1] In *The Hall* he refers to the effect of physical beauty; to a horse running down a soft, sloping plain; to a peacock displaying its own spring blossoms in its tail; to the sea; to an ant on the back of an elephant or camel; to the relative beauty of the voices of peacocks, nightingales and swans.[2] *A True Story* is a long fantasy

[1] Loeb Class. Lib. (London and New York 1913), vol. i, pp. 156, 162, 164.   [2] ibid., p. 178–96.

crammed with distorted botany, zoology and physiology.[1] In *Zeus Catechized*, Zeus himself hangs on a thread
like a fish on a line; a man throws a spear at a boar and
kills his friend; oaks and stones are struck by thunder-
bolts.[2] The list of Lucian's natural references could be
prolonged to a great many pages. The point to be made
is that despite the way in which his eye flickers obser-
vantly round everything in heaven and earth, he sees no
significance or meaning in what he sees. The gods are
put in their places with wicked malice; Fate rules; the
argument from design is disposed of with a few deft
touches.[3] Where there is sustained natural description,
as in *The Fly*, it is a rhetorical exercise. All is swift,
glancing, brilliant and shallow. With it we may contrast Marcus Aurelius, who also observes closely, but
who never fails to find significance in what he observes.
Here, all is serious, all meaningful, all is seen in the
light of his gentle, undogmatic Stoicism as part of a vast
enacted parable telling of the unity of all creation.
If there are moments when intellectual virtuosity gets
the better of a writer like Clement of Alexandria, or
when rhetorical flourish is dominant in an Oration
by Gregory of Nazianzus or a Homily by Basil, yet the
Greek fathers are at one with Marcus Aurelius rather
than with Lucian, not in respect of his world-weary
Stoicism, but in respect of the seriousness of his treatment of nature. The fathers saw nature not merely as a
convenient source of simile and metaphor (though they
did use it in this way) but more as an ordered system
which they felt revealed something more beyond itself.
They were not always systematic in their exposition of
this theme, but we may isolate three stages in their

[1] Loeb Class. Lib. (London and New York 1913), vol. i,
p. 258ff.
[2] ibid., vol. 2, pp. 66, 76, 80.
[3] ibid., p. 148f.

approach to the final inference of the existence and goodness of God.

First, there is their conviction that the whole of creation forms a single system. In proportion to the strength of Platonic influence upon a writer, the system may be treated as continuous from the inanimate right through to the rational, or as discontinuous, with man standing midway to link the two separate orders. But in either case creation is to be regarded as a single act of the divine will. We have in an earlier chapter noted Nemesius' view of the unity of creation. This is emphasised for him by the manifest diversity of existing things. Not only are men free-willing and therefore diverse in their actions,[1] but are distinct even in appearance. From the manner in which sub-human creatures appear to recognise each other, the same must be true at their level: jackdaws and crows recognise their kind in order to mate.[2] And yet there is a continuity running through the whole, from the inanimate mineral to the rational man, which links the whole.[3] A constant pattern is maintained by the movements of stars, seasons, day and night.[4] Long before Nemesius, Origen had expressed the unity of creation by describing the functioning of different parts of creation as though they were limbs of a single body, an image partly Stoic and partly Pauline in origin: 'I am of the opinion that the whole world ought to be regarded as some huge and immense animal, which is held together by the power and reason of God, as by one soul.'[5] Eusebius too uses Stoic terminology in saying that the

[1] *de nat. hom.*, xl.57.

[2] ibid., xlii.62.

[3] ibid., v.24; cf. Minucius Felix, *Octav.*, xvii.

[4] ibid., xlii.60.

[5] *de princ.*, ii.1.3; cf. Athanasius, *de incarn.*, xli, 'the Word of God is in the universe, which is a body, and has penetrated every part of it'. Marcus Aurel., vii.13, 'Say to yourself, I am a limb of the organised body of rational things.'

unity of creation is maintained by the natural sympathy obtaining between its diverse parts.[1] Gregory of Nazianzus writes that creation is 'a system and compound of earth and sky and all that is in them, an admirable creation indeed when we look at the beautiful form of every part, but yet more worthy of admiration when we consider the harmony and unison of the whole, and how each part fits with every other in fair order, and all with the whole, tending to the perfect completion of the world as a unit'.[2] Gregory even uses the divine trinity as an analogy of the unity in diversity of the cosmos.[3] Gregory of Nyssa speaks of the unity and variety of the universe,[4] and Theodore of Mopsuestia interprets the *groaning and travailing* of Romans viii.22 as primarily spiritual, but shared and participated in by the whole visible creation.[5] This metaphysical unity is reflected in the physical structure of the universe, which is seen by Basil to be symmetrical and balanced about the earth as its centre,[6] and which is treated at some length by Theodoret,[7] and by Dionysius of Alexandria in his fragmentary *de Natura*.

The universe functions according to laws of nature which are also laws of God, the physical aspect of Natural Law, the idea of which was developed on its ethical side by the Stoics. This is a point which the fathers make with some care, since the cultural setting in which they made the point was not that in which

---

[1] *Prae. Evang.*, iii.13. Stoic terminology lay conveniently to hand for Christian writers concerned with the unity of the cosmos. H. E. W. Turner, *The Pattern of Christian Truth* (London 1954), p. 452, notes its use in this connection by Tatian, Athenagoras and Theophilus of Antioch.

[2] *Orat.*, xxxviii.10.

[3] ibid., xl.41.

[4] *antirrhet. c. Eunom.* (= *c. Eunom.*, xii.b); *de infant.*

[5] *Comm. in Rom.*, P.G., 66.828b.

[6] *Hex.*, i.10.24b; ii.7.48a.

[7] *Graec. affect cur.*, iv.58–68.

Jesus had made it.[1] No first-century Jew, hearing
Jesus say that *the earth beareth fruit of herself*, would have
been led to think that the origin and source of such
natural growth was an impersonal force. The Jewish
mind would have attributed the growth to God. In the
Hellenistic world there was greater danger that laws of
nature could be taken to imply an impersonal *Natura*,
and the fathers are at some pains to indicate that though
each moment of growth is not directly caused by a
separate act of the divine will, natural law is ultimately
derived from such an act and is therefore divine law.
It is this point which Origen urges against Celsus,
who had argued that physical changes in bodies are not
to be attributed to God. On the contrary, writes Origen,
laws regulating the change of bodies were established in
the beginning by God,[2] and it is therefore in accordance with an original divine *fiat* of this kind that appar-
ently spontaneous changes take place, such as physiological changes in the human body at puberty,[3] the
movements of animals, plants, fire and water, and the
incitement to activity (φαντασίας) which impels a
spider to weave a web.[4] Eusebius boldly writes of
nature as the universal mother, but insists at once that
she is subject to God's command and obeys divine laws,
and denies any kind of spontaneous causation.[5] Eusebius had already treated the question of causation at
greater length in an earlier passage of the *Praeparatio*.
Events can occur for different reasons, he writes. For
example, they may be effects contingent upon primary
occurrences, which 'renders the structure of the whole,
complex and intricate', as may be observed in the interaction of body and soul in a single man. This interaction
prevents even the animal functions of the human body

[1] e.g. Mark iv.28.   [2] *c. Cels.*, iv.57.
[3] *Hom. in Exod.*, iv.8.
[4] *de princ.*, iii.1.3; cf. *Hom. in Jos.*, xxiii.3.
[5] *Prae., Evang.*, vii.10.3.

from being totally irrational, since soul affects body and soul is not irrational. It is not irrational Fate which controls the body; it is the body's nature to act thus; its functions are contingent upon its original construction by God. The rational part of man can be affected by old age and physical mutilation, and in its turn it can affect the body's desire for sexual intercourse, food and warmth. Further, says Eusebius, there are innumerable accidents of life which can affect a man from outside himself, such as food, change of temperature, sudden cold and heat, each working according to its own natural laws. The action of other human wills touches our own life, with the result that our own will 'is disturbed by a thousand external wills'. The whole complex of action and motive exists within the overall context of divine providence. Eusebius adds that it is not quite accurate to say that all occurrences are contingent upon the primary act of God, for there are occasions when God changes the consequences of an event to suit special occasions. Actions fall into three classes, Eusebius concludes: those freely willed by ourselves; those which take place according to natural law contingently upon the primary act of God; those which are accidental, imposed upon us by the contingent actions of external bodies. But all 'are included in the one law which proceeds from the counsel of God'. There is no room for true irrationality or for Fate.[1] Eusebius' remarks about the interaction of body and soul are akin to those of Nemesius, who, however, makes the point with greater anatomical and physiological precision.[2] The two writers are at one in identifying natural law with divine law, and it is in the light of this that we have to understand Nemesius when he says that the irrational functioning of the body works according to laws of nature, and when he contrasts a woman's freedom of

[1] *Prae. Evang.*, vi.6.
[2] *de nat. hom.*, xxvii.43.

will to determine her sexual behaviour with the behaviour of irrational creatures which copulate 'under the
working of nature'.[1]

Basil leaves no doubt about his view of the matter.
He writes to console Briso's widow on the death of her
husband with the assurance that physical death is the
common lot of man since the days of Adam, and urges
her not to be resentful at the laws of nature which
affect us all, but rather to accept the dispensation of
God.[2] The body dies, as it has grown, 'according to the
action of nature'.[3] God's command at creation becomes
a law of nature;[4] just as a top revolves by virtue of
its initial impetus, so the order of nature, finding its
principle (ἀρχή) in this first command, runs through all
time.[5] Divine law, once put into operation, ensures the
proper functioning of the physical world, regulating
the motion of a sphere rolling down a slope in accordance with the properties pertaining to the sphere and
the slope until the sphere is brought to rest on a flat
surface, and the motion of a human body through its
allotted span of years until it too is brought to rest.[6]
Like Eusebius, Gregory of Nyssa draws attention to the
psychical and physical complex which underlies an
event. In the birth of a child there is the sexual passion
in the begetting, the physical process of 'laying the
foundations for the birth of the living creature, the
building up of nutritive processes in the mother;
beneath all this is nature with her miraculous working,
and beneath nature is the will of God'.[7] With this basis
of divine will understood, one can speak of mechanical
laws of nature determining the heat inherent in fire,
the splendour of a sunbeam, the fluidity of water, the
tendency of a stone to fall,[8] and the spark latent in

---

[1] ibid., xxiii.41; xxv.42.   [2] *Ep.*, 302.
[3] *Ep.*, 296.   [4] *Hex.*, v.1.96a.
[5] *Hex.*, v. 10.116c.   [6] *Hex.*, ix.2.189bc.
[7] *c. Eunom.*, i.39.   [8] ibid., i.28; cf. xii.4.

flint.[1] Wording used by Gregory of Nazianzus at one point suggests that certain occurrences can be outside the sphere of divine will: 'You are distressed by your travels, and think yourself unsteady like a stick carried along by a stream; but, my dear friend, the travels of a stick are involuntary while your course is ordained of God.'[2] But such an interpretation of his words is corrected elsewhere by the assertion that 'our very eyes and the law of nature teach us that God exists and that he is the efficient and maintaining cause of things'.[3] It may appear at times as though human affairs are ruled by Fate—the Clementine *Recognitions* suggest the possibility[4] and Basil toys with the idea as he thinks of his protracted separation from Eustathius, only to reject it.[5] The fathers as a whole will have none of it.[6] Nor will they allow any suggestion of spontaneous creation. Eusebius refers scornfully to the 'all wise Greeks' who sought the cause of everything in irrational impulse and spontaneous motion,[7] and Basil rejects utterly the opinion of those who present the origin of heaven and earth as the spontaneous coming together of the elements.[8] Existence has its cause in God's creative act and is maintained by God's providence.

Providence, says Nemesius in a twofold definition, is the care that God takes of things that exist, and the purpose of God whereby all existing things receive their most favourable outcome.[9] The two senses of the word are not always clearly distinguished by other

[1] *in Hex.*, *P.G.*, 44.72cd.

[2] *Ep.*, 81.   [3] *Orat.*, xxviii.6.

[4] *Rec.*, i.28.   [5] *Ep.*, 1.

[6] e.g. Justin, *Apol.*, i.7; i.43; Nemesius, *de nat. hom.*, xl.57; Basil, *Hex.*, vi.5.128a–133c; Greg. Naz., *Orat.*, vii.7; Greg. Nyssa, *c. Fatum*, *P.G.*, 45.149cd; etc.

[7] *Prae. Evang.*, i.8.13; cf. Athanasius, *de incarn.*, ii.

[8] *Hex.*, i.1.4a.

[9] *de nat. hom.*, xliii.63.

writers, for providence is frequently the subject of
enthusiastic and lyrical outbursts in which careful
definition is not conspicuous. The sphere in which
providence is effective is held to be limitless, as is shown
by the widespread patristic opposition to Aristotle's
limitation of it to certain areas of the cosmos,[1] and by
the variety of events and activities in which providence
is described as being operative, ranging from oversight
of the majestic cycles of the heavenly bodies[2] to the
social organisation of human society[3] and details of
day-to-day life such as the choosing of a suitable
husband for one's daughter,[4] and extending to the
minutest anatomical details of animals and insects.[5]
This is a theme, moreover, which covers the whole
range of patristic literature from the apostolic fathers
onwards.[6] It is the subject of complete works such as
the *De Providentia* of Theodoret and the *Hexaemeron* of
Basil, and fills the whole of the sixth book of Theodoret's
Graecarum Affectionum Curatio. It is an element of major
importance in the thought of Origen,[7] and conse-
quently in that of others such as the Cappadocian
fathers who are at one or two removes his disciples. It
should be noted that providence is not seen as being
operative only in regard to the utility of nature, but
also in regard to its beauty.[8]

[1] Tatian, *Orat. ad Graec.*, ii; Athenagoras, *Suppl.*, xxv; Hip-
polytus, *Philosoph.*, vii.19; Clem. Alex., *Strom.*, v.14.105; Origen,
Hom. in Gen., xiv.3; Eusebius, *Theoph.*, ii.20; *Prae. Evang.*, xv.5;
Theodoret, *Graec. affect. cur.*, vi.7; Greg. Naz., *Orat.*, xxvii.10.

[2] Theodoret, *de prov.*, i; ii; Basil, *Hex.*, i.3; etc.

[3] Origen, *Hom. in Num.*, xxviii.3.

[4] Chrysostom, *Hom. in Coloss.*, xii.7.

[5] Origen, *c. Cels.*, iv.54.

[6] e.g. Clem. Rom., *ad Cor.*, xx.1–12; *Ep. ad Diognet.*, vii.2.

[7] Scholars who disagree on other points concerning Origen,
agree on the paramount importance of the conception of providence in Origen's system of thought; e.g. Hal Koch, *Pronoia und
Paideusis*, and J. Daniélou, *Origen*.

[8] Dionysius of Alex., *de natura*.

In face of this tremendous emphasis upon nature as a divinely-created and divinely-maintained system, what have the fathers to say of the evil inherent in nature? It is not our intention here to digress into discussion of human sin, but we cannot wholly dissociate fallen man from the cruelties of the animal world in which he lives, in so far as man is part of that world. Many of the fathers express their awareness of the problems created by wastefulness and cruelty in the natural world, apart from human sin and its immediate effects. Origen points out how immensely deep the problem extends: if bodily pain is to be included within the terms of the problem, then desire for food or sexual intercourse must be included, being caused by something lacking in the human body. It is not good enough to blame the devil for such desires and to leave it at that, for there is a physiological aspect of these matters as well as a moral aspect.[1] No trouble is to be regarded as accidental, he continues, even loss of property, imprisonment, or the deaths of those dear to us through the collapse of a house which crushes them. Such occurrences are not directly caused by God, and yet do not take place without him.[2] The existence of evil can be described as an effect of his work, just as shavings and sawdust are an effect of the carpenter's work, or rubbish lying around a building-site is an effect of the architect's.[3] The immediate cause of natural disasters, such as the blasting of vines and fruit trees and pestilence among cattle, is the malice of daemons, just as that of natural blessings is the beneficence of good daemons,[4] for daemons are given charge of the natural world, regulating the affairs of animals, plants, stars and heavens, rain and wind, fish and all creatures on earth.[5] 'The whole world is full of

[1] *de princ.*, iii.2.1–3.   [2] ibid., iii.2.6f.
[3] *c. Cels.*, vi.55.   [4] ibid., viii.31.
[5] *Hom. in Jer.*, x.6; *Hom. in Jos.*, xxii.3; cf. Justin, *Apol.*, ii.5;

angels.'[1] Origen thus attributes lunacy not to natural
causes but to the work of a maleficent daemon.[2] It is
clear to him that not all human ailments have their
root in the sinful will of man, since children are born
with deformities. He recognises the appalling moral
difficulty of such an event, and says that the soul has
entered its human body from a previous existence and
that physical deformity is the result of the soul's misuse
of freewill in that previous existence.[3]

Some of the Greek fathers show that they were faced
by the pastoral problem of dealing with particular
evils and disasters as they occurred. In face of the death
of a child, Gregory of Nyssa says that the dish of life
often seems to be flavoured only by astringent and
vinegary sauces. Some guests are removed early from
the table by the intervention of a beneficent providence,
and are thereby saved from the evils of gluttony later in
the meal.[4] Gregory of Nazianzus had the unenviable
task of deputising for his father, bishop of Arianzum,
in addressing a farming community whose crops had
been ruined by rain and hail. He is not much at his
ease in speaking of the cause of the disaster. Is it some
disordered and irregular motion or some misdirected
current of air that has caused it, some unreason in the
universe, as though there were no ruler of the world,
which is therefore borne along by chance? Or are these
disturbances and changes of the universe, which was
constituted and harmonised by God in the beginning,
directed by reason and order under the direction of
his providence? Whence come famines and tornadoes?
Is it a test for the righteous,[5] or punishment for the

Athenagoras, *Suppl.*, x; Tertullian, *Apol.*, xlvi. Note Nemesius'
acceptance of belief in nymphs, *de nat. hom.*, i.7.

[1] *Hom. in Ezek.*, i.7.   [2] *Hom. in Matt.*, xiii.6.

[3] *de princ.*, ii.9.3, 5, 7.   [4] *de infant.*

[5] A question to which Origen had already given an affirmative
answer, *de princ.*, ii.3.2.

ungodly? Gregory does not answer his own question, for his real solution of the problem, which he gives later, is not an answer to this question at all. At this point he merely comforts his hearers by bidding them think that God might have smitten them with something much worse than hail—smoke and fire and burning coals, for example.[1] Theodoret is concerned with the apparent uselessness of some parts of creation. Why did God create wild animals which contribute nothing to the life of man? His answer is that wild animals do in fact serve man in teaching man to imitate their skills; the spider, for example, teaches man how to trap his food. Wild animals can also be tamed to work for man.[2] Origen had said that the service done by leopards and wild boars is to exercise the manly character within us when we hunt them.[3]

These would have been admitted by their writers to have been no more than partial answers to specific problems and situations. The real solution offered by the fathers to the problem of evil nature lies elsewhere, and is not only their solution to the problem of evil and cruelty but also points to their final explanation of the significance of the whole natural order. In brief, their solution of the problem of cruelty is that good will triumph in the end. It is a moral problem, and only a moral solution will be found ultimately satisfying. But no ultimate moral triumph is possible in this present age. It can, by definition, only be achieved when the ultimate term of the divine purpose for the universe is reached. To be understood, the problem must be seen teleologically by the philosopher, eschatologically by the

[1] *Orat.*, xvi.5f. That Gregory's comfort is not quite as cold as sounds will be evident to those who have seen patients in hospital take heart at realising that their affliction is not the worst that could have happened. 'You can always see somebody worse off than yourself.'

[2] *de prov.*, v., *P.G.*, 83.569a; 629c–637c.

[3] *c. Cels.*, iv.78.

Christian. In saying that this seems to be the right
solution to the problem, we do not thereby have to
identify ourselves with the particular expressions of the
idea employed by individual writers. At its simplest, the
idea finds expression that however terrible the present
trouble may be, in the end evil will be overcome. Thus
Gregory of Nazianzus assures the ruined farmers that
when the end comes some of them will be welcomed by
the unspeakable light and the vision of the holy and
royal Trinity.[1] There is no attempt here to minimise
the present calamity; Gregory depicts it in striking
colours, emphasising it to the very people who had
suffered it, describing farmers with heavy hearts sitting
beside the grave of their ruined harvest.[2] It would be
empty comfort indeed to try to persuade them that
their distress was imaginary and that in the life to come
they would see that the evil they had resented and
feared had been only illusion, a failure to see clearly
at the time. What in fact Gregory does is to recognise
the evil for what it is and then to assure the sufferers that
in the end there is victory. The same point is made
by Origen, taking up the theme of Romans viii.18ff.[3]
Do not imagine, he says, that earthly troubles can be
greater than the glory which shall be revealed. Pains
inflicted from within or without, the sufferings of Job,
tortures of mind and body—compared with eternity the
worst and longest suffering in this life is but momen-
tary and easy to bear.[4] So too, writing on the Psalms,
Origen says,

There are things in creation hard to understand, or even
undiscoverable for human beings. We are not in consequence to condemn the Creator of the universe just because

---

[1] *Orat.*, xvi.9.

[2] ibid., xvi.6.

[3] *For I reckon that the sufferings of this present time are not worthy to be
compared with the glory which shall be revealed to usward* (R.V.).

[4] *Comm. in Rom.*, vii.4.

we cannot discover the reason for the creation of scorpions or other venomous beasts. The right thing for a man who is aware of the weakness of our race and who knows it is impossible to understand the reasons of God's design even when most minutely examined, is to ascribe the knowledge of these things to God, who will later on, if we are judged worthy, reveal to us the matters about which we are now reverently in doubt.[1]

This is a slightly different point, that the defect lies in human apprehension, to be dispelled by perfect vision. There are Platonic overtones here which suggest intellectual satisfaction without being quite convincing that the moral difficulty will also be resolved.

But the fathers are not content to rest on the assurance of an after life. Nature itself must be viewed teleologically: it points forward to an end, and is constructed in such a way as to lead the eye forward, as it were, from the partial to the complete, from the lower natural orders to the higher. Origen will have nothing of Celsus' attempts to deflate the superiority accorded to man by Christian teaching. From an examination of the history of animals and of their wisdom, writes Celsus, it seems as likely that things came into existence for their sake as for the sake of man. Rain exists as much for the sake of plants as for man. Against this Origen asserts a clear hierarchy within nature; all things are primarily for man, secondarily for the irrational animals, then for the plants that supply the needs of the animals.[2] His principle is that the lower order can only be understood in relation to its end. To understand the plant one must look to the animal; to understand the animal one must look to man; to understand man one must look to God. Gregory of Nyssa is saying something close to this in his analysis of the three types of soul, vegetative, animal and rational, all three of which man possesses,

[1] *Select. in Psalm.; philocalia* ii.
[2] *c. Cels.*, iv.74f.

being the culminating point of creation. After inanimate matter was created, writes Gregory, as a kind of foundation for what was to follow, vegetative life followed, then animals, man last. 'Thus nature advanced in an orderly course to perfection.'[1] So too, Nemesius describes the hierarchy of nature progressing from inanimate things, through plants and animals to man,[2] and Basil, following a rather different path, moves through the lower orders to the bodily and mental superiority of man.[3] The principle is that which is expounded pastorally by Gregory of Nazianzus, that the part is to be understood in terms of the whole, the beginning in terms of the end, the imperfect in terms of the perfect.

A third form of the teleological view of nature has for its starting point the seminal words of Paul, 'the earnest expectation of the creation waiteth for the revealing of the sons of God. For the creation was subjected to vanity, not of its own will, but by reason of him who subjected it, in the hope that the creation also shall be delivered from the bondage of corruption into the liberty of the glory of the children of God' (Romans viii.19–21, R.V.). The fathers knew their scriptures well enough to be aware that writers many centuries earlier than Paul had also expressed the idea of a final regeneration of the natural order, notably Isaiah xi.6–9; but Paul seems to be the focus of the idea. It is possible that we find a hint of it in the Epistle of Barnabas, which describes fallen man undergoing a new creation in Christ prior to being led to a land flowing with milk and honey; but this land may symbolise the spiritual kingdom of God upon earth and not a regeneration of the natural order.[4] Irenaeus is more specific, quoting Isaiah xi and continuing:

I am quite aware that some persons endeavour to refer these words to the case of barbarians of different nations

---

[1] *de hom. opif.*, viii.4–7.   [2] *de nat. hom.*, i.3.
[3] *Hex.*, ix.2.192a.   [4] Barnabas, *Ep.*, vi.

and various customs who come to believe. . . . But although
this is true, nevertheless in the resurrection of the just the
words shall also apply to the animals mentioned. For God is
rich in all things. And it is right that when the creation is
restored, all animals should obey and be in subjection to
man and revert to the food originally given by God (for
they had been originally subjected in obedience to Adam),
that is, the products of the earth.[1]

Theophilus of Antioch bases his belief in the restoration
of animals upon Romans viii. When animals had been
created, he says, God saw that they were good; it is
man's fault that they are bad. They fell with man, just
as servants follow their master. With man also they will
be restored.[2] Origen's theory of successive physical
restorations has earned him criticism; even so loyal a
disciple as Gregory of Nyssa deserts his master at this
point. It is, moreover, difficult to pin Origen down to a
specific statement that there will be restoration of the
non-rational elements of the universe. In an exposition
of Psalm 102.26 he writes that if the heavens are to be
changed like a vestment, then they are not to be destroyed, 'and if the fashion of the world passes away, it
is by no means an annihilation or destruction of their
material substance that is shown to take place, but a
kind of change of quality and transformation of appearance'. It is primarily of physical human bodies that he
is writing, as the continuation of the passage makes
clear, but it is hard to exclude other material bodies
from his meaning.[3] The change will be to a purity like
the aether. In a later passage he writes, 'When the end
has been restored to its beginning and the termination
of things compared with their commencement, that
condition of things will be re-established in which
rational nature was placed when it had no need to eat
out of the tree of the knowledge of good and evil.'[4]

[1] adv. haer., v.33.4.   [2] ad Autol., ii.17.
[3] de princ., i.6.4.   [4] ibid., iii.6.3.

This again could refer not only to man but also to man's physical environment, a restoration of Paradise. During the series of restorations through which more and more rational beings will have returned to God, successive restorations also of the physical universe will be necessary. When all have returned, at the point when God is all in all, the whole creation will also have returned to a permanent state of aetherial purity.[1] Gregory of Nyssa recognises only a single restoration when 'a hymn of thanksgiving will arise from all creation'.[2] Chrysostom reverts to the imagery of Theophilus: creation was corrupted on man's account, bringing forth thorns and thistles. With man it will again become incorruptible, clothed with a brighter garment in honour of man's deliverance, just as a father clothes his servants suitably when his son achieves some new dignity.[3] This is the time when the wolf shall dwell with the lamb and the leopard shall lie down with the kid, when creation shall be delivered from the bondage of corruption into the liberty of the glory of the children of God, the time which creation awaits with earnest expectation. This is the time when the cruelty of nature shall be seen to have been no mere illusion, but a dark reality now overcome.

Further, the restoration of nature will have its focus in the glorified Christ. This idea also has its origin in a passage of Paul, where he writes of the Father's will 'to sum up all things in Christ, the things in the heavens, and the things upon the earth' (Ephesians i.10). It is not simply that at the end all creation will be handed over to the Son to rule,[4] but that every stage of nature's

[1] ibid., ii.10.8. The idea that Origen taught a restoration of the physical senses of man is disputed by J. Daniélou, *Platonisme et théologie mystique* (2nd ed., Paris 1954), and *Origen* (Eng. tr., London and New York 1955), p. 307f.

[2] *Orat. cat.*, xxvi.

[3] *Comm. in Rom.*, xiv (Rom. viii.21).

[4] Origen, *de princ.*, iii.5.6. This is perhaps as far as we should

physical development and man's spiritual development
will be summed up in him who will be the end term
of the whole immeasurably great process. Hippolytus
writes: 'This Word we know to have received a body
from a virgin, and to have remodelled the old man by
a new creation. And we believe the Word to have
passed through every period of this life, in order that he
might himself serve as a law for every age.'[1] The idea
is put strongly by Irenaeus:

Jesus Christ gathered together all things in himself. But in
every respect, too, he is man, the formation of God; and
thus he took up man into himself, the invisible becoming
visible, the incomprehensible being made comprehensible,
the impassible becoming capable of suffering, and the Word
himself being made man, thus summing up all things in
himself. So that as in supercelestial, spiritual and invisible
things the Word of God is supreme, so also in things visible
and corporeal he might possess supremacy, and taking to
himself the pre-eminence, as well as constituting himself
head of the Church, he might draw all things to himself
at the proper time.[2]

It was this that had been foretold by the prophets when
they said that a new thing would come to give renewal
and life.[3]

Two points arise out of this: first, that if the glorified
Christ is to include and sum up in himself the whole of
creation, then he must be really and organically part
of that creation; secondly, that in the earthly ministry
of the incarnate Word, a foretaste of the end is given.
In view of the first of these two points, it is clear at once
that the disputes of the first few centuries of the Christian era concerning the nature of Christ's person and
status were not the wasteful wrangles over theological

press Justin's picture of Christ in majesty as Lord of all, *Dial.*,
lxxv.

[1] *Philos.*, x.33.
[2] *adv. haer.*, iii.16.6.   [3] ibid., iv.34.1.

minutae which to some they seemed at the time, and
have seemed since. It was vital to 'place' Christ in
relation to the natural and the divine with the utmost
possible precision. To the Greek fathers it was of the
first importance to maintain the real humanity of
Christ, for unless he was part of humanity he could not
sum it up in himself, but would remain a divine visitor
from outside, coming or going, staying or absenting
himself, but never organically part of the world of men
and animals and trees and rocks. Origen, who has been
castigated for paying too little attention to the incarnate
Christ, saw very clearly the importance of real incarnation. 'We do not for a minute forget the incarnation,'
he wrote, 'even at the height of contemplation.'[1] There
was constant warfare against gnostic and docetic tendencies to minimise the true humanity of Christ, and
constant attention to the narratives of the historical
events of the ministry, expressed in homilies and com-
mentaries on the gospels, in the creeds and in the liturgy
of the Church. It was felt that to lose touch with this
reality would be to lose the salvation of man and the
fulfilment of God's purpose for the whole natural order,
which waited with earnest expectation for the revealing
of the sons of God (Romans viii.19). It was of equal importance to maintain the true divinity of the incarnate
Word, without which perfect salvation and fulfilment
would again be unattainable. To this end the fathers
stood against attempts made to define the status of the
divine Word in terms of creation. However great the
created being, created however long before the rest
of creation, salvation could be achieved only by the
divine. Man stands midway between the irrational
and the rational orders, belonging to both and linking
them; Christ stands midway between the irrational
and rational creation on the one hand and the divine
on the other, belonging to both and linking them. The

[1] *Comm. in Joh.*, ii.8.

effect of this upon the natural order will only be seen at the end, when the full purpose of God is revealed and evils vanquished. But, for the moment, we have been given a glimpse of the end. The incarnate Jesus of Nazareth is a sacrament of the glorified Christ who will at the end sum up all things in himself.[1] It is at this point that the Christian, having seen in the person of Jesus what nature can lead to, is able to turn back to the phenomena of nature and see them in a new light. In the light of Christ he can see nature in terms of its divinely-appointed end, and therefore cannot be satisfied with any partial view of it. We have seen above that the Greek fathers have little good to say of science. It is not necessarily that they think the scientific view of any given phenomenon is wrong in fact, for often, having written slightingly of science as a whole, they go on to use the work of earlier scientists and pursue the study of phenomena in considerable detail as far as their knowledge permits them. What they will not allow is the idea that the scientific view is the whole view. To those who have seen a glimpse of the fulfilment of nature in Christ, the scientific view is manifestly not the whole, though it may be helpful and is certainly interesting. The whole view—what Gregory of Nazianzus called the 'knowledge of the realities themselves'[2]— is the view seen in terms of purpose and end, and the end, teleologically and chronologically alike, is Christ.

This point is made by Origen.

All the things in the visible category can be related to the invisible, the corporeal to the incorporeal, the manifest to those that are hidden; so that the creation of the world itself, fashioned in this wise as it is, can be understood through the divine wisdom, which from actual things and

---

[1] Origen, *de princ.*, iv.3.13.
[2] *Orat.*, xxviii.29, cited above, p. 4.

copies teaches us things unseen by means of those that are seen, and carries us over from earthly things to heavenly.[1]

There is here a two-way interaction of material and spiritual: the material can only be understood in the light of the spiritual, and yet we can approach the spiritual by means of the material, just as in the study of the scriptures the historical can only be understood fully in the light of the spiritual, and yet the approach to the spiritual is through the historical.

We know that in its work of creation the divine skill is displayed not only in the heavens and in sun and moon and stars, as it pervades the whole of their mass, but also on earth it operates in the same way in any common substance, so that the bodies of the tiniest animals have not been neglected by the Creator. Far more is this true of the souls that exist in them, each soul receiving some special property, the saving element in the material. It is so in the plants of the soil; in each is an element of design, affecting its rocks and leaves and the fruit it can bear and the characteristics of its qualities. Now we take the same view of all scriptures that proceed from the inspiration of the Holy Spirit. . . . He who has once accepted these scriptures as the work of Him who created the world must be convinced that whatever difficulties in regard to creation confront those who strive to understand its system, will occur also in regard to the scriptures.[2]

And the method by which Origen treats scriptural difficulties corresponds to that by which he treats those of the natural world. Fr. H. de Lubac, in a study of Origen's exegetical method,[3] denies the accusation often made against Origen that he neglects the historical sense of scripture. The same is true of Origen's understanding of the universe; he does not neglect the

[1] *Comm. in Cant.*, iii.2.

[2] *Select., in psalm: philocalia*, ii. Tr. R. B. Tollinton (London 1929).

[3] *Sources chrétiennes*, 16, Intro., p. 35f.

I

physical, but sees it as one element in a greater whole, an element whose significance simply does not exist until its end is achieved. Christ, says Fr. de Lubac, does not in Origen's view *show* the spirituality of the Law: he *creates* it by his cross and resurrection. Without this illumination the whole Jewish cult is nothing, mere empty decoration;[1] so nature before Christ is empty, mere decoration, until its meaning is created for it by Christ. Prophecies of Christ only become prophecy after Christ has fulfilled them;[2] so also it is only in Christ that the created universe receives meaning.

Seen from this vantage point in Christ, what significance does nature reveal? In the first place, the Greek fathers see it to have allegorical significance; that is, it can be taken piece by piece and translated into its spiritual equivalent. In this region of simile, which is neglected by few of the fathers, we are at the mercy of the literary ability of each writer. Animals are constantly allegorised, with some consensus of opinion about what is symbolised by each animal. Clement of Alexandria interprets the young of various animals and birds—lambs, calves, pigeons and doves, colts, chickens and young asses—to signify various kinds of innocent and childlike mind.[3] Elsewhere, while writing on the Christ-Orpheus theme, Clement examines the symbolism of animals tamed by the 'new song': birds, the frivolous; reptiles, the deceivers; lions, the irascible; swine, the voluptuous; wolves, the rapacious.[4] Much of this symbolism is common property to all. Origen, however, regards the horse as the symbol of voluptuous living,[5] and to Barnabas the hare, hyaena and weasel signify various kinds of sexual malpractice.[6] Barnabas lists and explains in turn the clean and unclean crea-

---

[1] *Comm. in Cant.*, i.2.   [2] *Comm. in Joh.*, i.8.

[3] *Paed.*, i.15.14.   [4] *Protrept.*, i.4.1.

[5] *Hom. in Jesu Nave*, xv.3.

[6] *Ep.*, x.6–8; cf. Clem. Alex., *Paed.*, ii.10, on hare and hyaena.

tures of Leviticus,[1] the details of his interpretation differing little from those employed throughout succeeding centuries.[2] There was, however, scope here for originality of treatment. While Theophilus of Antioch regards sea monsters and carnivorous birds as meaning the strong who devour the weak,[3] Origen takes them to signify evil thoughts.[4] But Theophilus is afraid of the implications of his essay in allegorisation and hastens to say that he regards Eden as a real place 'towards the East . . . beneath our skies',[5] whereas Origen, who was quite ready to admit his fallibility in allegorising, would never shrink from an inference once he was sure of his ground, and boldly says that we may take Adam to mean mankind as a whole.[6] The fathers were not confined to biblical imagery. Hypocritical Christians are like mad dogs which bite secretly;[7] Christians cower before the emperor like birds cowering before an eagle;[8] the devil devastates the Church like a wild boar among the crops;[9] the townsfolk of Cappadocian Caesarea rush from their work like bees driven from their hive by smoke;[10] Christ descended upon the daemons and philosophers like a lion upon foxes;[11] sin is still active in man, like the writhing tail of a snake after its head has been struck;[12] those who live in reliance upon magic and astrology are living in darkness, dull and blind like moles.[13] Nor are the fathers confined to animal

---

[1] *Ep.*, x.4f.

[2] e.g. Origen, *de princ.*, iv.1.8; *c. Cels.*, iv.50; Euseb., *Comm. in Is.*, xi.6; xxxiv.15; *Dem. Evang.*, ii.3.111; Theodoret, *de prov.*, v., *P.G.*, 83.628cd.

[3] *ad Autol.*, ii.16.   [4] *Comm. in Gen.*, i.8–9.

[5] *ad Autol.*, ii.24.   [6] *c. Cels.*, iv.40.

[7] Ignatius, *ad Ephes.*, vii.1.   [8] Basil, *Ep.*, 145.

[9] Gregory Naz., *Orat.*, xlii.41.

[10] ibid., xlii.57.

[11] Chrysostom, *Comm. in Rom.*, xxxii (Rom. xvi.24).

[12] Greg. Nyssa, *Orat. cat.*, xxx.

[13] Clem. Alex., *Protrept.*, xi.115.3.

symbolism. Hermas constantly allegorises natural objects of all kinds. To Theophilus of Antioch the law and the prophets come with mercy and justice like a river of fresh water running into the salt sea;[1] and the fixed stars represent prophets while the planets represent men of wandering mind.[2] Clement of Alexandria sees truth veiled like reflections in water,[3] and heretics as being bitter inside like wild almonds.[4] Eusebius constantly allegorises water and the sea.[5] To Basil good deeds can be blotted out by evil deeds like dust settling on the surface of a pool.[6] Gregory of Nyssa dismisses the ideas of Eunomius by comparing them to air bubbles among falling water, but even so the orthodox stand silent before his impiety like physicians standing helpless before a cancer.[7] Self-indulgence spreads like a film over an eye.[8] One passion affects the whole soul like ripples spreading all over a pond.[9] Gregory, writing of the incarnation, describes deity enveloping human flesh like flame enveloping a burning substance.[10] Cyril of Jerusalem sees the effects of sin remaining in the soul like a scar remaining after a wound.[11] Chrysostom often uses snow as a symbol: temptations fall thick as snowflakes;[12] Paul's miracles came thick as snow;[13] Paul's dangers came upon him thick as snowflakes.[14] Chrysostom describes people who praise you to your face and mock you in secret as being like children who crown each other with crowns of grass and then run out of sight to giggle.[15] This kind of allegorical reference to nature is found throughout patristic writings. Only

[1] *ad Autol.*, ii.14.   [2] ibid., ii.16.
[3] *Strom.*, v.9.56.5.   [4] ibid., vii.16.99.5.
[5] *Comm. in Is.*, xxxv.7; *Comm. in Psalm.*, lxiv.7; lxxvi.19; lxxxviii.9; xcii.3.
[6] *Ep.*, 42.   [7] *c. Eunom.*, vii.1f.
[8] *de virg.*, x.   [9] ibid., xiv.
[10] *Orat. cat.*, x.   [11] *Cat.*, xviii.20.
[12] *Comm. in Rom.*, ii; xxxi.   [13] ibid., xxix.
[14] ibid., xvi.   [15] ibid., xvii.

occasionally, as in the case of Basil and Theodore of
Mopsuestia, do we find deliberate opposition to allegorisation, but their opposition is more concerned with
historical truth than with nature. 'I take everything at
its face value,' declares Basil,[1] writing about the creation narrative; but even so he has recourse to allegory
when it suits him. The simple equation of natural
objects with spiritual can be effective, but it is a wholly
personal, individual literary device, depending upon
the ability of the writer to observe accidental points of
similarity or identity in the two objects compared. The
similarities are in any case accidental, in the philosophical sense, and do not indicate any essential unity between the objects, although there may on occasions be
a unity which goes deeper than accidental similarity,
akin to the unity between type and anti-type in the
historical sphere.

When nature reveals this kind of deeper unity with
spiritual reality it exhibits what the fathers call an
anagogue (ἀναγωγή) of the world of the spirit. The idea
is familiar to us as part of the technique of scriptural
exegesis that Origen adopted from Philo and expounds
in *De Principiis* iv. Every passage of scripture is a
mystery,[2] which can be unfolded to reveal truths of
general (mystical) application or truths of individual
(moral) application. It is clear that every natural object
can be treated allegorically according to the whim of
the individual, but texts of scripture narrate historical
incidents which have a forward reference to later and
more significant incidents. The crossing of the Red Sea
by the Israelites prefigures Christian baptism for
Origen in a sense which links type and anti-type much
more intimately than can be designated by the terms
simile or allegory. It is not simply that the crossing of
the Red Sea is 'like' baptism: it is rather that the

[1] *Hex.*, ix.1.188c; cf. iii.9.73d–76a.
[2] *Hom. in Gen.*, x.1.

actual meaning of the crossing was hidden until the institution of baptism revealed it. One moves historically forward from the crossing of the sea to baptism, and then theologically back again to see the crossing in a new light. The two belong together, though separated chronologically, just as one might see a man's shadow before seeing the man himself. Certain natural phenomena appear to have this kind of two-way reference in patristic writings. Perhaps the clearest, and one of the commonest, is the way in which rebirth in nature is seen as an anagogue of the resurrection of the body. Clement of Rome sees the natural anagogue of resurrection in the appearance of day after night, in fruit springing from seed and in the phoenix legend.[1] Theophilus of Antioch sees it in the emergence of new days and new seasons, in the germination of seed, in the waxing of the moon and in the recovery of the human body from sickness.[2] Origen sees it in the growth of plants from seed.[3] Cyril of Jerusalem sees it in the blossoming of a pruned tree and the sprouting of a transplanted vine.[4] There is possibly not a patristic writer who produced a considerable body of work who does not draw attention to the principle of resurrection in the natural world. The point is that it is a principle, part of the structure of nature, and no mere illustration in which heterogeneous objects are placed side by side for comparison. It is thus possible to argue straight from nature to the spiritual, and then to pass back to nature with new understanding of its significance in this respect. An image which may perhaps be associated with the resurrection anagogue, and which is employed far beyond the bounds of patristic literature, is that of the passing of beauty. The fragility of the blossom reminds Basil, as it does Chrysostom, of the shortness of human life

[1] *ad. Cor.*, xxiv. 3–5; xxv. 1–4.
[2] *ad Autol.*, i.13; ii.16.
[3] *c. Cels.*, v.18.   [4] *Cat.*, xviii.6.

upon earth.[1] Human life, says Gregory of Nazianzus, is like passing dreams, like the flight of a passing bird, like a ship leaving no track upon the sea, a speck of dust, a vapour, an early dew, a flower that quickly blooms and quickly fades.[2] *Où sont les neiges d'antan?* This group of images is part of the tradition of civilised man, not of the fathers only; and indeed the sadness of the theme may find expression less in the fathers than elsewhere, being extinguished in their minds by the greater strength of the resurrection anagoge. More important to the fathers, if we may judge by the frequency of its employment, is a closely-knit group of images concerning light and heat which are held to demonstrate the nature of the Godhead. We are not here concerned with the orthodoxy or otherwise of the doctrine approached by means of this anagogue, which is employed by writers of many shades of theological opinion. The natural phenomenon observed is that a ray of light is in a relation of closest possible intimacy with its source, but yet remains distinct from its source. This takes the form sometimes of a sunbeam in relation to the sun, sometimes a ray of light from a lamp, sometimes of the light and heat emitted from the sun, sometimes the heat emitted from white-hot iron, and is used to demonstrate the relationship of Father to Son, or of the three persons of the Trinity.[3] The writers are arguing directly from the structure of nature to that of the Creator. The type of argument employed is seen to advantage in Gregory of Nyssa's *Great Catechism*, though he is here arguing not from the structure of matter but

[1] Basil, *Hex.*, v.2.97c; Chrysostom, *ad Eutrop.*, *P.G.*, 52.393.

[2] *Orat.*, vii.19.

[3] Tatian, *Orat. ad Graec.*, v.1; Origen, *de princ.*, i.2.4; Athenagoras, *Suppl.*, x.3; Hippolytus, *c. Noet.*, x; xi; Eusebius, *Dem. Evang.*, iv.3.2; iv.3.7; *de eccles. theol.*, i.8.3; Apollinarius, *Frag.*, 124; Athanasius, *Orat. c. Ar.*, i.11.37; *Ep. de decr. Nic.*, v.23.10f; Greg. Nyssa, *c. Eunom.*, i.36; Greg. Naz., *Orat.*, xxxi.31f, finds the symbolism unsatisfactory; Chrysostom, *Hom. in Joh.*, iv.2; etc.

from human nature. His own description of the process
is that he is moving 'anagogically (ἀναγωγικῶς) from
matters that concern ourselves to that transcendent
nature'.[1] The relationship of lower to higher is closely
akin to that between type and anti-type in the historical
sphere, and just as in the latter sphere the existence of
such a relationship depends upon different historical
events being seen as linked parts of a single process, so
in the natural sphere the existence of an anagogical
relationship between material and spiritual depends
upon different objects being seen as linked parts of a
single system. It is because the fathers see the universe
thus that they can pass in a moment from the material
to the spiritual in worship, and back again to the
material in rich appreciation and enjoyment of its
beauty.

The danger here is pantheism, where the passage
between the material and the spiritual is made with
such ease that the distinction between the two becomes
blurred. It is a danger which the Greek fathers do not
fail to guard against. 'God is spirit,' writes Tatian, 'not
pervading matter, but the maker of matter and of the
forms that are in matter.'[2] Athenagoras distinguishes
carefully between Creator and creation: 'The world
is certainly beautiful, wonderful in its size as in its
orderly arrangement . . . yet we worship the Creator,
not the creation. I admire its beauty and worship its
Creator.'[3] Clement of Alexandria worships 'that beauty
which is the archetype of all that is beautiful', and goes
on to add that our image of the divine is not a sensory
image of sensible matter, but an image that is per-
ceived by the mind alone.[4] 'It is the Lord of the winds
that I long for, the master of fire, the maker of the
universe, him who lighted up the sun. I seek God, not

[1] *Cat. magn.*, ii.   [2] *Orat. ad Graec.*, iv.
[3] *Suppl.*, xvi; cf. xv.
[4] *Protrept.*, iv.49.2; iv.51.6.

the works of God.'¹ A symbol which is too beautiful can distract the mind from what is symbolised, and can lead, as Gregory of Nazianzus points out, to idolatry. It is better to use the beauty and order of visible things to attain that beauty which is beyond sight, and not to suffer the loss of God through the splendour of visible things.² The man of half-formed intelligence, says Gregory of Nyssa, when he observes an object which is bathed in the glow of apparent beauty, thinks that the object is in its essence beautiful and goes no deeper. A more developed mind will see outward beauty as the ladder by which he climbs to that intellectual beauty from which all other beauties derive their existence and their names in proportion to their share in it.³ The danger of a too-beautiful symbol is that it can by its beauty impede the passage of the mind, for anagogical thinking is a movement of the mind between two poles in the manner described by Gregory of Nyssa. The mind can remain so absorbed by the beauty of the material pole that the movement to the spiritual becomes frozen.

The Greek fathers, for all their intense appreciation of nature, for all their interest in the structures and processes of nature and their insistence upon nature as a means by which God reveals his nature, nevertheless hold that God and nature are not identical, and that the mind must penetrate nature to find God. The beautiful, the useful, the intellectually fascinating, even the spiritually beneficial—all these characteristics of nature can, if allowed to become an end in themselves, distract the mind from its proper activity, the knowledge of God. Nature must not be permitted to make too great demands which might impede the forward movement of understanding. From this arises the tension, which is characteristic of Christanity from the New Testament onwards, between deep appreciation

¹ ibid., vi.67.2.   ² *Orat.*, xxviii.13.
³ *de virg.*, xi.

of nature on the one hand and a refusal on the other hand to be side-tracked or delayed by its beauty. The fathers follow the New Testament closely in exhibiting a disturbing oscillation between world acceptance and world renunciation. 'Consider the lilies of the field' is followed soon by the stern reminder that 'here we have no continuing city'. The tension is real and may not be minimised. Detachment from this world is demanded often and uncompromisingly by Origen[1] and yet he never shuts his eyes to the beauty of the world around him. Gregory of Nyssa urges the necessity of rising above nature[2] and yet he loves the beauty that lies around him. The resolution of the tension may lie in this, that the man who is freed from the demands of nature is free to enjoy it fearlessly. Freed from it, Basil and Nemesius can return to it to probe its structures and processes with whatever assistance they can obtain from Aristotle or Theophrastus or Galen; Clement of Alexandria can return to enjoy the everyday things of country life; Gregory of Nyssa can love the sight of children playing with sunbeams and building sand castles, and can retread the ground already covered by Basil, gleaning here and there what his great brother had missed. We find here in varying degrees of intensity the combined love of nature and detachment from its demands which was later, in the figure of Francis of Assisi, to kindle the imagination of Europe.

[1] e.g. *Comm. in Matt.*, xii.5; *Hom. in Num.*, xxvii.12.

[2] *de orat. dom.*, ii; *de beat.*, vi; See J. Daniélou, *Origen* (Eng. tr., London and New York 1955) part 4.

Bibliography of Patristic Sources

1 *Apostolic Fathers* (late first, early second century)
Clement of Rome, *Epist.*, 1; pseudo-Clement (= Clem. Rom., *Ep.*, 2); Barnabas, *Epist.*; Papias, *Fragments*; *Epist. ad Diognetum*; Ignatius of Antioch, *Epistulae*; Hermas, *Pastor*.
All in *Patrum Apostolicorum Opera*, O. Gebhardt, A. Harnack, Th. Zahn (ed. minor, Leipzig 1877).

2 *Greek Apologists* (second century)
Justin, *Apologies*, i and ii; *Dialogue with Trypho*; Tatian, *Oratio ad Graecos*.
Athenagoras, *Supplicatio; de Resurrectione.*
All in E. J. Goodspeed, *Die ältesten Apologeten* (Göttingen 1914).
Theophilus of Antioch, *ad Autolycum*, Migne, *P.G.*, 6.
Irenaeus, *adversus Haereses*, Migne, P.G., 7.

3 *Alexandria and Egypt*
Clement of Alexandria (late second century)
    Protrepticus and *Paedagogus*, G.C.S., 12; *Stromateis*, G.C.S., 15, 17; *Quis Dives Salvetur? G.C.S.*, 17.
Origen (late second, early third century)
    Homily on Genesis, S.C. 7; *Hom. on Jeremiah*, G.C.S., 6; *Hom. on Exodus*, S.C. 16; *Hom. on Numbers*, S.C., 29; *Hom. on Joshua*, S.C., 71; *Hom. on Canticles*, G.C.S., 33; *Commentary on Matthew*, G.C.S., 40; *Comm. on John*, G.C.S., 10; *Comm. on Canticles*, G.C.S., 33; *contra Celsum*, G.C.S., 2, 3; *de Principiis*, G.C.S., 22.
Hippolytus of Rome (early third century)
    Philosophumena, G.C.S., 26.
Dionysius of Alexandria (third century)
    apud Eusebius, *Hist. Eccles.*, vii, *G.C.S.*, 9.2.

Athanasius (fourth century)
  Discourses against the Arians, Migne, *P.G.*, 26; *Apology against the Arians*, Migne, *P.G.*, 25.
Pseudo-Athanasius (late fourth century)
  de Incarnatione, Migne, *P.G.*, 26.
Synesius of Cyrene (late fourth, early fifth century)
  Hymns, Migne, *P.G.*, 66.

4 *Cappadocia*
Basil of Caesarea (late fourth century)
  Homilies on the Hexaemeron, *S.C.*, 26; *Epistulae*, ed. R. Deferrari (Loeb Classical Library).
Gregory of Nazianzus (late fourth century)
  Orations, Migne, *P.G.*, 35, 36; *Epistulae*, Migne, *P.G.*, 37.
Gregory of Nyssa (late fourth century)
  Explicatio; *Apologetica in Hexaemeron*, Migne, *P.G.*, 44; *de Beatitudinibus*, Migne, *P.G.*, 44; *adversus Eunomium*, Migne, *P.G.*, 45; *contra Fatum*, Migne, *P.G.*, 45; *Oratio Catechetica Magna*, Migne, *P.G.*, 45; *de Virginitate*, Migne, *P.G.*, 46; *Sermons on the Forty Martyrs*, Migne, *P.G.*, 46; *Praise of the Martyr Theodore*, Migne, *P.G.*, 46; *de Opificio Hominis*, *S.C.*, 6.

5 *Antioch and Syria*
Eusebius of Caesarea (late third, early fourth century)
  De Vita Constantini, *G.C.S.*, 7; *Historia Ecclesiastica*, *G.C.S.*, 9.1, 2; *Theophany*, *G.C.S.*, 11.2; *Demonstratio Evangelica*, *G.C.S.*, 23; *Praeparatio Evangelica*, *G.C.S.*, 43.1, 2; *Commentary on the Psalms*, Migne, *P.G.*, 23, 24; *Comm. on Isaiah*, Migne, *P.G.*, 24; *contra Marcellum*, Migne, *P.G.*, 24.
Cyril of Jerusalem (fourth century)
  Catechetical Lectures, Migne, *P.G.*, 33.
Nemesius of Emesa (late fourth century)
  de Natura Hominis, Migne, *P.G.*, 40.
John Chrysostom (late fourth century)
  de Incomprehens. Dei, *S.C.*, 28; *Commentary on Romans*, Migne, *P.G.*, 59.
Theodore of Mopsuestia (late fourth, early fifth century)
  Catechetical Homilies, ed. R. Tonneau and R. Devresse (*Studi e Testi* 141, Rome); *Comm. on the Minor Epistles of Paul*, ed. H. B. Swere (Cambridge 1880–2).

Macarius of Magnesia (*c.* 400)
  Apocritica, ed. C. Blondel (Paris 1876).
Theodoret of Cyrrhus (early fifth century)
  Graecarum Affectionum Curatio, *S.C.*, 57; *de Providentia*,
  Migne, *P.G.*, 83.

Where applicable, use has been made of the English
translations of the *Ante-Nicene Christian Library* (Edin-
burgh 1864ff), the *Ante-Nicene Fathers* (Grand Rapids,
Michigan), the *Nicene and Post-Nicene Fathers* (Grand
Rapids, Michigan), the *Library of Christian Classics*
(Philadelphia and London) and the *Loeb Classical
Library* (London and Cambridge, Mass.).

Bibliographical note on
Secondary sources

On the pagan background the fullest treatment is still that of A. Biese, *Die Entwicklung des Naturgefühls bei den Griecher und Römern* (Kiel 1882–4) and *Die Naturgefühl im Mittelalten und in der Neuzeit* (revised ed., Leipzig 1888). Also useful are W. R. Hardie, 'Feeling for Nature in the Greek and Roman Poets' (*Lectures on Classical Subjects*, London, 1903); H. R. Fairclough, *Love of Nature among the Greeks and Romans* (New York 1930); E. R. Dodds, *Pagan and Christian in an Age of Anxiety* (Cambridge 1965), especially pp. 1–36; R. A. Norris, *God and World in Early Christian Theology* (London 1966).

On ancient scientific thought there are a number of historical outlines: L. Thorndike, *A History of Magic and Experimental Science* (London 1923), especially Vol. 1, Chap. 21; A. J. Brock, 'Galen on the Natural Faculties' (*Loeb Classical Library*, London and New York 1916), Introduction; C. Singer, *A Short History of Science* (Oxford 1941), especially pp. 32–128; *A History of Biology* (revised ed., New York, 1950), especially pp. 1–62; *Evolution of Anatomy* (London 1925) for its treatment of Galen; Benjamin Farrington, *Greek Science* (London 1944). A. Harnack, *Medicinisches aus der ältesten Kirchengeschichte* (*Texte und Untersuch.* viii. 4, Leipzig 1892) is good, particularly on the Latin side.

On particular patristic writers there is much that has been written about their philosophical antecedents which, though not central to the theme of this study, is in general terms important: for Justin, W. Schmid, Frühe Apologetik und Platonismus (*Festschrift Otto Regenbogen*, 1952, p. 163ff); for I Clement, G. Bardy, 'Expressions stoiciennes dans la Iᵉ Clementis' (*Récherches de Science réligieuse* 12, 1932); for Theophilus of Antioch, J. Geffcken, *Zwei griechischen*

Apologeten (Leipzig 1907); for Clement of Alexandria,
O. Schilling, *Reichtum und Eigentum in der altkirchlichen Literatur*
(Freiburg im B. 1908), pp. 40–7; M. Spanneut, *Le Stoicisme
et les Pères de l'Église de Clém. Rom.* (*Patristica Sorbonensia* 1;
Paris 1957); G. Verbeke, *L'Evolution de la Doctrine du Pneûma
du Stoicisme à Saint Augustin* (Louvain 1945); A. Decker,
Kenntnis und Pflege des Körpers bei Klemens von Alexandrien
(Innsbruck 1936); for Origen, G. Bardy, 'Origène et la
magie' (*Récherches de Science réligieuse* 18, 1928); H. Koch,
Pronoia und Paideusis (Leipzig 1932); E. de Faye, *Origène*
(Paris 1923–8), especially Vol. 2; J. Daniélou, *Origen*
(English tr., London and New York 1955); R. B. Tollinton,
Alexandrian Teaching on the Universe (New York 1932); for
Basil, K. Gronau, *Poseidonios und der jüdischchristliche Gene-
sisexegese* (Leipzig-Berlin 1914); S. Giet, *Les idées et l'action
sociales de saint Basile* (Paris 1941); P. J. Levie, *Les Sources de
la 7me et de la 8me Homélies de saint Basile sur l'Hexaémeron*
(Musée Belge 1914 (1920)); J. Courtonne, *Saint Basile et
l'Hellénisme* (Paris 1934); for Gregory of Nyssa, J. Daniélou,
Platonisme et Théologie Mystique (Paris 1944); for Nemesius,
W. W. Jaeger, *Nemesios von Emesa* (Berlin 1944); E. Skard,
Nemesios-studien 1 (*Symbolae Osloenses*, xv, Oslo 1936);
F. Lammert, *Zur Lehre von den Grundeigenschaften bei Nemesios*
(*Hermes*, lxxxi, pp. 488–91, Wiesbaden 1953); for Theodore
of Mopsuestia, H. Kihn, *Theodor von Mopsuestia und Junilius
Africanus als Exegeten* (Freiburg im. B. 1880); R. Devresse,
Essai sur Théodore de Mopsueste (*Studi e Testi*, 141, Vatican
City, 1948); R. A. Norris, *Manhood and Christ* (Oxford 1963).

The Introductions and Notes appended to texts of the
Greek fathers are useful on particular points, especially
those of *Sources chrétiennes* (= *S.C.*). For Theophilus of
Antioch, G. Bardy in *S.C.*, 20; for Clement of Alexandria,
Paedagogus, H-I. Marrou in *S.C.*, 70; *Protrepticus*, Claude
Mondesert, S.J., in *S.C.*, 2.2; *Stromateis*, Marcel Caster in
S.C., 30; for Origen, *Homiles on Exodus*, H. de Lubac in
S.C., 16; for Basil, *Hexaemeron*, Stanilas Giet in *S.C.*, 26;
for Nemesius, W. Telfer, *Nemesius of Emesa on the Nature of
Man* (Lib. of Christian Classics, iv, London 1955); for
Gregory of Nyssa, *de opificio hominis*, J. Daniélou in *S.C.*, 6.

Index of patristic writers

Index of non-Christian writers

Index of subjects